The Lorette Wilmot Library
Nazareth College of Rochester

Detroit Studies in Music Bibliography, No. 79

Editors
J. Bunker and Marilyn S. Clark
University of Kansas

The Theater Music of Samuel Arnold:

A Thematic Index

by

Robert H. B. Hoskins

HARMONIE PARK PRESS
WARREN, MICHIGAN
1998

Frontispiece:
"The Harvest Home"
From *The Tour of Dr Syntax in Search of the Picturesque* (1812), by William Combe
Illustration by Thomas Rowlandson, pen and watercolor over pencil
Courtesy of author

Copyright 1998 by Harmonie Park Press
Printed and bound in the United States of America
Published by
Harmonie Park Press
23630 Pinewood
Warren, Michigan 48091

Editor, J. Bunker Clark
Book design, Elaine J. Gorzelski
Typographer, Colleen McRorie

Library of Congress Cataloging-in-Publication Data

Hoskins, Robert H. B.
    The theater music of Samuel Arnold : a thematic index / by Robert H. B. Hoskins.
       p.   cm. — (Detroit studies in music bibliography ; no. 79)
    Includes bibliographical references (p.   ) and index.
    ISBN 0-89990-082-8
    1. Arnold, Samuel, 1740-1802—Thematic catalogs. 2. Dramatic music—Thematic catalogs. I. Title. II. Series
ML134.A78A2   1998
782.1'092—dc21   97-46479

For Cecily and Polly,

with love

Contents

Illustrations   *ix*

Music Examples   *xi*

Acknowledgments   *xiii*

Chronology of Samuel Arnold   *xv*

Guide to Thematic Index   *xxi*

Select Bibliography   *xxiii*

Abbreviations   *xxv*

Theater Works of Samuel Arnold   *xxvii*

The Theater Music of Samuel Arnold: A Thematic Index

Introduction   3

A Thematic Index   57
  A / *All-Sung Operas*   57
  B / *Mainpiece Operas with Spoken Dialogue*   62
  C / *Afterpiece Operas with Spoken Dialogue*   93
  D / *Pasticcios and Other Operas with Contributions by Arnold*   120
  E / *Pantomimes*   136
  F / *Incidental Music*   153

Index of Text Incipits   159

Illustrations

"The Harvest Home"	*frontispiece*
Samuel Arnold, 1795	*xiv*
Samuel Arnold holding his edition of *Cathedral Music*, 1790	*xvii*
Samuel Arnold, 1803	*xix*
Samuel Arnold in his doctoral robes, 1797	2
John O'Keeffe, Irish dramatist	4
George Colman, the elder	4
George Colman, the younger	4
The Haymarket Little Theatre and its successor, the New Haymarket Theatre, 1831	5
The Haymarket Little Theatre in the 1790s	5
The rustic setting of *The Maid of the Mill*, as conceived by John Inigo Richards	9
Title-page of *The Castle of Andalusia* keyboard-vocal score, November 1782	11
Elizabeth Bannister, *née* Harper, Arnold's star soprano	12
Libretto of *Inkle and Yarico*, August 1787, with frontispiece showing Yarico "discover'd asleep" at the entrance of her cave	20
Cartoon depicting Prince William Henry as Trudge with Wowski in *Inkle and Yarico*	20
Sarah Harlowe as Adeline disguised as a soldier in *The Battle of Hexham*	21
John Edwin as Lingo the schoolmaster-butler woos Mary Wells as Cowslip the dairymaid in *The Agreeable Surprise*	31
Page from Harrison's keyboard-vocal score of *Peeping Tom*	34
Frederick and Mary Menage sing the "bird" duet in the original production of *The Children in the Wood*	35
The Children in the Wood, John Bannister as Walter agitated by Josephine's sad song "The Norfolk Tragedy"	36
Title-page of *The Shipwreck*, after Samuel James Arnold?	40
Arnold's autograph manuscript of the beginning of Venture's song for Dibdin's *The Seraglio*, 1776	42
Hester Colles in the title role of *Polly*	44
James Graham and Gustavus Katterfelto, whose cure-alls touch the buffoonery in *The Genius of Nonsense*, 1780, and *None Are So Blind as Those Who Won't See*, 1782	47
Maria DeCamp as Rosa sings a "Spanish" guitar-song to Charles Kemble as Jack, act 2, *Obi: or, Three-Finger'd Jack*	50

Music Examples

1.	*The Portrait*, no. 4, meas. 28-36	6
2.	*The Portrait*, no. 3, meas. 39-47	7
3.	*The Enraged Musician*, no. 21, meas. 23-36	7-8
4.	*The Maid of the Mill*, **B1.1**, meas. 1-17	10
5.	*The Castle of Andalusia*, **B5.6**, meas. 20-23	11
6.	*The Castle of Andalusia*, **B5.11**, meas. 14-18	12
7.	*The Siege of Curzola*, no. 8, meas. 88-92	13
8.	*The Spanish Barber*, no. 4, meas. 10-32	13-14
9.	*The Spanish Barber*, no. 11, meas. 9-16	14
10.	*The Spanish Barber*, no. 6, meas. 81-89	15
11.	*The Spanish Barber*, overture, "El Fandango," meas. 1-6	15
12.	*Two to One*, no. 1, meas. 12-20	16
13.	*Two to One*, no. 14, meas. 104-13	16
14.	*Turk and No Turk*, no. 2, meas. 53-62	17
15.	*Turk and No Turk*, overture, first movement, meas. 1-12	17
16.	*Inkle and Yarico*, no. 12, meas. 13-18	18
17.	*Inkle and Yarico*, no..3, meas. 25-30	18-19
18.	*Inkle and Yarico*, no. 6, meas. 15-19	19
19.	*The Battle of Hexham*, no. 1, meas. 9-16	21-22
20.	*The Battle of Hexham*, no. 9, meas. 5-11	22
21.	*The Battle of Hexham*, no. 4, meas. 14-19	22-23
22.	*The Surrender of Calais*, no. 7, meas. 41-44	23
23.	*The Mountaineers*, overture, first movement, meas. 1-9	23
24.	*Zorinski*, no. 1, meas. 17-20	24
25.	*Zorinski*, no. 2, meas. 9-12	24
26.	*Cambro-Britons*, no. 7, meas. 12-17	25
27.	*The Enchanted Wood*, overture, first movement, meas. 1-6	26
28.	*The Son-in-Law*, no. 5, meas. 50-57	26
29.	*The Son-in-Law*, no. 7, meas. 13-24	27

30.	*The Dead Alive*, no. 7, meas. 31-50	28
31.	*The Agreeable Surprise*, overture, first movement, meas. 1-4	29
32.	*The Agreeable Surprise*, no. 5, meas. 41-52	29
33.	*The Agreeable Surprise*, no. 7, meas. 54-76	30
34.	*Gretna Green*, no. 14, meas. 66-99	32-33
35.	*Peeping Tom*, no. 3 (complete tune)	33
36.	*The Children in the Wood*, no. 5, meas. 18-25	36
37.	*The Children in the Wood*, no. 8 (complete tune)	37
38.	*The Children in the Wood*, no. 4, meas. 1-14	37
39.	*Auld Robin Gray*, no. 13, meas. 17-28	38
40.	*The Shipwreck*, no. 1, meas. 26-39	38-39
41.	*The Shipwreck*, no. 2, meas. 1-10	39-40
42.	*The Summer's Tale*, **D2.6**, meas. 61-69	41
43a.	*The Seraglio*, **D6.1**, meas. 46-56	41-42
43b.	Charles Dibdin, *The Padlock* (London: author, [1768]), p. 18, meas. 1-8	42
44.	*Polly*, **D7.20e**, meas. 1-4	43
45.	*Polly*, **D7.6e**, meas. 1-4	43
46.	*Polly*, **D7.20d**, meas. 1-4	44
47.	*Polly*, **D7.2**, meas. 9-16	45
48.	*Polly*, act 3, no. 10, meas. 9-12	45
49.	*Mother Shipton*, no. 24, complete	46-47
50.	*The Genius of Nonsense*, no. 21, meas. 31-35	48
51.	*Obi*, no. 8, meas. 1-11	49
52.	*Obi*, no. 8 (cont.), meas. 14-17	49
53.	*Obi*, no. 46, complete	51
54.	*Obi*, no. 12, Andante, meas. 13-20	52
55.	*The Corsair*, no. 50, meas. 22-47; no. 51, meas. 1-4	52-53
56.	*Fairies' Revels*, no. 12 (= overture, second movement), meas. 1-8	53
57.	*Macbeth*, **F1.6**, meas. 1-8	54

Acknowledgments

The officers of the several libraries in which I have worked have been invariably helpful, and I am particularly grateful to Peter Ward Jones and Robert Bruce of the Music Room in the Bodleian Library and the assistants in the British Library.

J. Bunker Clark is a model of all general editors; his many suggestions and criticisms have been invaluable, and his patience exemplary.

Research for this volume was begun during a period of study leave, spent in Oxford, from Massey University, Palmerston North. I gratefully acknowledge the Faculty of Humanities and the Publications Committee at Massey University for help of so many kinds, and also to Keble College, Oxford, for electing me a Senior Visiting Member in 1990, so making the time there more productive. I also owe a large debt of another kind to my wife Cecily.

ROBERT H. B. HOSKINS

Massey University
New Zealand

SAMUEL ARNOLD

Pencil sketch by George Dance, dated 25 January 1795.
Courtesy National Portrait Gallery

Chronology of Samuel Arnold

1740 (August 10 [new style])	Born in Westminster, son of Thomas Arnold, a commoner, and the Princess Amelia (?).
ca. 1750-58 (August 31)	Receives musical education as a Child of the Chapel Royal; possibly noticed by Handel.
1758-64	An organist in various London churches; writes songs "gratis" for Vauxhall Gardens.
1764 (March 4)	Admitted as a professional member of the Royal Society of Musicians; becomes a member of the Court of Assistants from 1765 and elected a Governor, 21 June 1767 (the first of three terms).
1764 (autumn)	Engaged by John Beard as harpsichordist and composer to Covent Garden.
1765 (January 31)	*The Maid of the Mill*, his theater début, performed at Covent Garden with acclaim.
1767 (January 23)	*The Cure of Saul*, the first of Arnold's four early oratorios, performed at the King's Theatre.
1768-73	Directs Lenten oratorio concerts (sometimes together with Edward Toms) at Drury Lane; also 1776-77 and (together with Thomas Linley, Sr.) 1786-93.
1769-74 (October)	Proprietor of Marylebone Gardens; concerts typically include a staged miniature opera followed by fireworks. Also writing numerous keyboard works and songs published singly and in collections. A rogue employee creates heavy financial loss, forcing Arnold to sell the Gardens.
1770	Begins collaboration with George Colman, the elder, in *The Portrait* (November 22).
1771	Marries Mary Ann Napier, heiress (?).
1773 (April 14)	Directs a performance of *The Jesuit* (partly musical setting of George Marriott's religious allegorical poem) at the Crown and Anchor tavern.

CHRONOLOGY OF SAMUEL ARNOLD

1773 (July)	Takes the Bachelor of Music and Doctor of Music at Oxford (July 3); oratorio *The Prodigal Son* performed at the Sheldonian Theatre as part of the festivities when Lord North is installed as chancellor of Oxford University (July 8).
1774	Samuel James Arnold born. Begins liaison with Miss Hook (3 children ?).
1777	Engaged by Colman, the elder, as composer and music director for the Haymarket Little Theatre; *Polly*, with new music by Arnold, produced (June 19); also *The Spanish Barber* (August 30).
1778	Caroline Arnold born (dies 13 December 1795). The birth dates of Arnold's two other daughters, ? and Marianne, untraced. Arnolds living at 22 Charlotte Street, Rathbone Place.
1781 (September 4)	*The Agreeable Surprise* performed at the Haymarket Little Theatre with enduring success.
1782	Living in Great Pultney Street. Writes three short keyboard concertos "for the ease of beginners." *The Castle of Andalusia* performed at Covent Garden (November 2); appeals for the use of popular modes—comic, sensational, and melodramatic.
1783 (March 1)	Becomes organist and composer to the Chapel Royal; writes anthems that exploit his command of Handel's style.
1783-86	Serves as editor (together with Thomas Busby) of *The New Musical Magazine* (ca. 1783-86) and *Harrison's New German-Flute Magazine* (1784-85). Becomes a reviewer in the *European Magazine* (1784-?) and writes the musical chapter in Daniel Fenning's *The Young Man's Book of Knowledge* (1786 ed.).
1784	Patents a new type for music printing (April 24). Serves on the Concert Committee of the Royal Society of Musicians (June 20), which was involved in Handel Commemoration concerts (repeated in subsequent years).
1786-97	Working on edition of Handel's works, issued in 180 parts, but far from definitive in terms of its inclusiveness or textual authority.
1787 (August 4)	*Inkle and Yarico* performed at the Haymarket Little Theatre; regarded as the first anti-slavery opera.

Samuel Arnold holding his edition of Cathedral Music

Engraving by John Russell, 1790.
Courtesy Bodleian Library

1787 (December 22)	Establishes the Glee Club at the Crown and Anchor tavern, with John Wall Callcott and others; serves as president until 1797 (?).
1789 (August 11)	*The Battle of Hexham*, the first of the Arnold-Colman (the younger) experimental hybrid operas, performed at the Haymarket Little Theatre.
1789-94	Conductor of the Academy of Ancient Music (fortnightly concerts during the winter); specializes in performances of Handel.
1790 (November)	Founds the Graduates Meeting, a society of academic musicians (November 24); they meet monthly for supper at one another's houses. Publication of a four-volume continuation of Boyce's *Cathedral Music*.
1791	Directs a performance of *Redemption* (Handel pasticcio arranged by Arnold) at the Chapter House, Canterbury Cathedral (August 16). Meets Haydn at the Graduates Meeting (October 26). First Choral Fund annual concert

	(December 5), established by Arnold for ailing musicians and their families (writes an *Ode to Charity* for the Fund in 1798). *The Psalms of David* (compiled together with Callcott) published (December 8).
1791-94	President of the Anacreontic Society (meets fortnightly during the winter at the Crown and Anchor tavern).
1792	Arnold unwell with gout (January). Directs Royal performance of Handel's *Messiah* at St. Margaret's Church (May 31; Haydn invited to play harpsichord continuo but for some reason declines). Arnold reports to Chapel Royal Fund subscribers on feasibility of benefit concerts (December 27).
1793	A long-standing Freemason, Arnold begins to direct the societies' annual concert-in-aid of female orphans (April 23). Becomes organist to Westminster Abbey (September 29; installed 14 June 1796). *The Children in the Wood* performed at the Haymarket Little Theatre (October 10).
1794	Fails in a bid to lease the Lyceum Theatre for operatic productions (his son obtains the lease in 1815). *Auld Robin Gray* (libretto by his son) performed at the Haymarket Little Theatre (July 26; Haydn attends an early performance).
1795	Conducts choruses from the organ for Salomon's new Opera Concert subscription series at the King's Theatre; Haydn at the harpsichord (February-May). Arnold offers to include a Haydn symphony in the Freemason's charity concert (March 20); Haydn refuses "since they wouldn't have any rehearsal."
1797 (May 24)	Arnold begins to conduct the annual performance at St. Paul's Cathedral for the benefit of the Sons of the Clergy.
1798 (autumn)	Arnold falls from a stepladder in his library, snaps a tendon in his leg and suffers internal injuries, from which he never recovers.
1800 (July 2)	*Obi: or, Three Finger'd Jack* performed at the Haymarket Little Theatre; Arnold's pantomime raises the issue of racial difference.
1801	Conducts Lenten oratorio concerts at the Haymarket Little Theatre, including Haydn's *Creation* (March 6) and his own *Elisha* (March 13). Issues a prospectus for a new revised edition of Handel's works (winter).

CHRONOLOGY OF SAMUEL ARNOLD

1802	Completes his "creation" oratorio *The Hymn of Adam and Eve* (January 20; unperformed). *Fairies' Revels*, his last theater work, performed at the Haymarket Little Theatre (August 14). Health deteriorates; dies at home, 22 Duke Street, Westminster (October 22); buried in the north aisle of Westminster Abbey (October 29); trustees of the Chapel Royal Fund pay £49 assurance to his widow.
1803	Samuel James Arnold's portrait of his father published posthumously (March). Arnold's effects sold at a four-day auction (May 24-27). Arnold dies intestate; the administration of his goods and chattels (£2000) granted to his widow (December 6).

SAMUEL ARNOLD

Engraving by William Ridley, 1803,
after the original by Samuel James Arnold.
Courtesy Bodleian Library

1812	On the death of Mary Ann, authority to administer Arnold's estate granted to his son (December 31).
1830	Arnold's fame and infectious good spirits recalled in a memoir provided by William Ayrton (?).

Guide to Thematic Index

Design

The purpose of this index is to list the complete theater music of Samuel Arnold, including within each entry that information beneficial to librarians and students for the identification of the repertory and the special characteristics of the sources in which it is preserved. Capital letters distinguish the main divisions of the repertory. Numbers identify works. Numerical suffixes, following a dot, can be used to identify movements within a work. These numbers may be used to express overlapping relationships.

The listing of works has six main categories, which are distinguished by the following alphabetic prefixes:

> A / *All-sung operas*
> B / *Mainpiece operas with spoken dialogue*
> C / *Afterpiece operas with spoken dialogue*
> D / *Pasticcios and other operas with contributions by Arnold*
> E / *Pantomimes*
> F / *Incidental music*

Works within each category are listed chronologically. The format of each entry provides space for the registration of the following elements:

- Index number with title, alternative title.

- Genre identification and number of acts.

- Librettist and sources.

- London theater and date of first performance.

- Listing of manuscript, keyboard vocal score and supplementary scores, with sources and notes relative to the specific publication (publisher, year of issue, date of issue entered at Stationer's Hall, opus number, RISM print number).

- List of singing characters with names of performers. Gender identification arranged by order of the text incipits.

- Musical incipits. An incipit for each instrumental movement and for the first vocal entry of each section of the work is given. A separate incipit for each entry is given for the incidental music, works in which the music is mostly not extant, additional songs, and numbers Arnold contributed to pasticcios and other operas. For pantomimes, an incipit for the first movement of the overture and for the first vocal or instrumental entry of each section is given. For vocal incipits, introductory measures of instrumental music have been excluded, but the number of excluded measures is indicated. In works of multiple voices or instruments, the entry of the highest voice provides the incipit, but in some instances fuller harmonic material is accommodated. The entering voice is identified in all circumstances in which it might otherwise be unclear. Tempo and character designations are included.

- Text incipits. Listings of text incipits are provided for all vocal entries, including recitatives, arias and ensembles (abbreviations: Qt = Quartet, Qnt = Quintet, Sxt = Sextet, Chos = Chorus, Fnle = Finale). All first lines are given, usually preserving text repetition, along with the character names. Spelling and elisions generally respect the usage in the original score (sometimes discrepancies occur even between the libretti and musical settings of them). Punctuation and accents have been standardized to clarify basic understanding. The majority of commas added for grammatical reasons mirror rests in the music. The comments in editorial brackets [ ] supply information about borrowings (for example, references to folksong and citations from other composers), contributions by other composers, vocal resources, and instrumentation. An incipit marked with an asterisk (*) is also published separately, and readers are referred to my dissertation listing of printed sources and the RISM print number. Incipits marked with a cross (+) have a known manuscript source cited in the commentary. For pantomimes, instrumental numbers as well as vocal are listed, along with tempo, key, meter, and scenario.

- Commentary. The comments supply information about the music, performances, editions of the music, manuscript material, libretto and song-words, literary and historical commentaries, and archival resources. Comments may clarify discrepancies and correct misinformation in existing literature on Arnold. The musical discussion is intended as a preliminary survey—an assessment of Arnold's intentions and achievements.

SELECT BIBLIOGRAPHY

The only full-length study of Samuel Arnold is my Ph.D. dissertation, "Dr. Samuel Arnold (1740-1802): An Historical Assessment" (University of Auckland, 1982); volume 1 is biography and criticism, including a systematic study of the theater music, and volume 2 is a work-list and thematic catalog. Studies relating to Arnold's stage works include Roger Fiske's monumental *English Theatre Music in the Eighteenth Century* (London: Oxford University Press, 1973, reprinted 1986), my chapter "Theatre Music II" (1760-1800), in *The Blackwell History of Music in Britain*, 4: *The Eighteenth Century*, ed. H. Diack Johnstone and Roger Fiske (Oxford: Blackwell, 1990), 261-312, and my article "The Pantomimes and Ballets of Samuel Arnold," *Studies in Music* 14 (University of Western Australia, 1985): 80-93. Writings on individual theater works by Arnold include my introduction to *The Castle of Andalusia* (referenced under **B5**), and in *Obi: or, Three Finger'd Jack* (with Eileen Southern, referenced under **E9**), my article "Samuel Arnold's *The Spanish Barber*," *Early Music New Zealand* 4 (1985): 11-14, and Susan L. Porter's introduction to *The Children in the Wood* (referenced under **C18**), and her "'Children in the Wood': The Odyssey of an Anglo-American Ballad," in *Vistas of American Music: Essays and Compositions in Honor of William L. Kearns*, ed. Porter and John Graziano (this publisher, 1998). Other Arnold studies are J. M. Coopersmith, "The First Gesamtausgabe: Arnold's Edition of Handel's Works," *Notes* 4 (1947): 227-91, 438-39, my "Samuel Arnold's Keyboard Sonatas: A Commentary and Index," *Studies in Music* 25 (1991): 53-72, and Eva Zöllner, "Israel in Babylon or The Triumph of Truth? A Late Eighteenth-Century Pasticcio Oratorio," *Consort* 51 (1995): 103-17. Patrick J. Rogers, "A Bibiographic Survey of Arnold's Handel Edition, the first *Gesamtausgabe*" is in *Music in Performance and Society: Essays in Honor of Roland Jackson*, ed. Malcolm Cole and John Koegel (this publisher, 1997). The *New Grove* (1980) article is by Roger Fiske, with worklist by myself; this will be updated in the forthcoming revised edition. The *New Grove Opera* (1992) article is mine.

A number of studies relating to Arnold and his theater music are referenced under the List of Abbreviations (p. 25) and in the commentaries to individual works. The main ones are Burnim, *Colman 1*; Busby, *Anecdotes*; Colman, *Random Records*; Link, *O'Keeffe*; O'Keeffe, *Recollections*; Tasch, *Colman 2*; and Oulton, *Theatres*. Mention should also be made of ABC Dario Musico (Bath: author, 1780), "Biographical Sketch of the Late Dr. Arnold," *Monthly Mirror* 10 (1803): 147-52, 225-26; "Memoir of Samuel Arnold, Mus. Doc.," *Harmonicon* 8 (1830): 137-41 (probably by William Ayrton, Arnold's son-in-law); William Scrope Ayrton, *Memoir* [1876] and *Correspondence of Marianne Ayrton, ca. 1793-1834* (Ms., Library of Congress); [William Bingley], *Musical Biography*, 2 vols. (1814; rev., London: Colburn, 1834; reprint, New York: Da Capo, 1971); John Genest, *Some Account of the English Stage from the Restoration in 1660 to 1830*, 10 vols. (Bath: Carrington, 1832); Jane Girdham, *English Opera in Late Eighteenth-Century London: Stephen Storace at Drury Lane* (Oxford: Clarendon, 1997); J. Sainsbury, publisher, *A Dictionary of Musicians from the Earliest Ages to the Present Times*, 2 vols. (London, 1824; another impression, 1825, reprinted, New York: Da Capo, 1966); *The Thespian Dictionary: or, Dramatic Biography of the Eighteenth Century, Containing Sketches of the Lives, Productions, &c. &c. of All the Principal Managers, Dramatists, Composers* (London: T. Hurst, 1802, revised 1805); Linda Troost, "The Rise of English Comic Opera, 1762-1800" (Ph.D. diss., University of Pennsylvania, 1985); and Michael Winesanker, "Musico-Dramatic Criticism of English Comic Opera, 1750-1800," *Journal of the American Musicological Society* 2 (1949): 87-96.

Major secondary bibliographies are Eric Walter White, *A Register of First Performances of English Operas and Semi-Operas from the 16th Century to 1980* (London: Society for Theatre Research, 1983), and H. Diack Johnstone's exhaustive listing of books, dissertations, and occasional manuscript items in *The Blackwell History of Music in Britain*, 4: *The Eighteenth Century* (Oxford: Blackwell, 1990), 474-521.

ABBREVIATIONS

Burnim, *Colman 1*	Kalman A. Burnim, ed., *The Plays of George Colman, the Elder*, 6 vols. (New York and London: Garland, 1983).
Busby, *Anecdotes*	Thomas Busby, *Concert Room and Orchestra Anecdotes, of Music and Musicians, Ancient and Modern*, 3 vols. (London: Clementi, 1825).
Colman, *Random Records*	George Colman, the younger, *Random Records*, 2 vols. (London: Bentley, 1830).
Fiske, *Theatre Music*	Roger Fiske, *English Theatre Music in the Eighteenth Century* (London: Oxford University Press, 1973; reprint, 1986).
Gooch and Thatcher	Bryan N. S. Gooch and David Thatcher, *A Shakespeare Music Catalogue*, 5 vols. (Oxford: Oxford University Press, 1991).
Hoskins, *Arnold*	Robert Hoskins, "Dr Samuel Arnold (1740-1802): An Historical Assessment," 2 vols. (Ph.D. diss., University of Auckland, 1984).
Landon, *Haydn*	H. C. Robbins Landon, *Haydn: Chronicle and Works*, vol. 3: *Haydn in England, 1791-95* (London: Thames and Hudson, 1975).
Larpent	Ms. plays and libretti submitted for censorship by the Lord Chamberlain's office, now in the Huntington Library, San Marino, California. References to catalog number cited in Dougald MacMillan's *Catalog of the Larpent Plays in the Huntington Library* (San Marino: Huntington Library, 1939).
Link, *O'Keeffe*	Frederick M. Link, ed., *The Plays of John O'Keeffe*, 4 vols. (New York and London: Garland, 1981).
London Stage	*The London Stage, 1660-1800: A Calendar of Plays, Entertainments, and Afterpieces*, 5 pts. in 11 vols. (Carbondale: Southern Illinois University Press, 1960-68). Part 4: 1747-1776, ed. George W. Stone, Jr., 3 vols. (1962); part 5: 1776-1800, ed. Charles B. Hogan, 3 vols. (1968).

Music for London Entertainment — *Music for London Entertainment, 1660-1800* (Tunbridge Wells: Richard Macnutt, 1983-87; London: Stainer & Bell, 1988-). References to series, volume, page.

Nineteenth-Century American Musical Theater — *Nineteenth-Century American Musical Theater*, 16 vols. (New York and London: Garland, 1994). Reference to vol. 1, *British Opera in America: Children in the Wood (1795) and Blue Beard (1811)*, ed. Susan L. Porter (1994).

O'Keeffe, *Recollections* — John O'Keeffe, *Recollections of the Life of John O'Keeffe, Written by Himself*, 2 vols. (London: Colburn, 1826).

Oulton, *Theatres* — Walley C. Oulton, *A History of the Theatres of London from 1771 to 1795*, 3 vols. (London: Martin and Bain, 1796).

PMLA — Publications of the Modern Language Association of America.

RISM — *Répertoire international des sources musicales* (Munich and Duisberg, 1960-; Kassel, 1971-).

Tasch, *Colman 2* — Peter A. Tasch, ed., *The Plays of George Colman, the Elder*, 2 vols. (New York and London: Garland, 1981).

THEATER MUSIC OF SAMUEL ARNOLD

A / *All-Sung Operas*

A1	ROSAMOND (1767)
A2	THE ROYAL GARLAND (1768)
A3	THE SERVANT MISTRESS (1770)
A4	THE REVENGE (1770?)
A5	APOLLO TURNED STROLLER (1770?)
A6	THE PORTRAIT (1770)
A7	THE MAGNET (1771)
A8	THE CURE FOR DOTAGE (1771)
A9	DON QUIXOTE (1774)
A10	THE WEATHERCOCK (1775)
A11	APRIL DAY (1777)
A12	THE ENRAGED MUSICIAN or UT PICTORIA POESIS! (1789)

B / *Mainpiece Operas with Spoken Dialogue*

B1	THE MAID OF THE MILL (1765)
B2	THE SPANISH BARBER or THE FRUITLESS PRECAUTION (1777)
B3	SUMMER AMUSEMENT or AN ADVENTURE AT MARGATE (1779)
B4	BARON KINKVERVANKOTSDORSPRAKINGATCHDERN (1781)
B5	THE CASTLE OF ANDALUSIA (1782), an alteration of THE BANDITTI (1781)
B6	TWO TO ONE (1784)
B7	TURK AND NO TURK (1785)
B8	THE SIEGE OF CURZOLA (1786)
B9	INKLE AND YARICO (1787)
B10	THE BATTLE OF HEXHAM or DAYS OF OLD (1789)
B11	NEW SPAIN or LOVE IN MEXICO (1790)
B12	THE SURRENDER OF CALAIS (1791)
B13	THE ENCHANTED WOOD (1792)
B14	THE MOUNTAINEERS (1793)
B15	ZORINSKI (1795)
B16	THE ITALIAN MONK (1797)
B17	CAMBRO-BRITONS (1798)
B18	FALSE AND TRUE or THE IRISHMAN IN ITALY (1798)

C / Afterpiece Operas with Spoken Dialogue

- C1   THE MADMAN (1770)
- C2   LILLIPUT (1777)
- C3   THE GIPSIES (1778)
- C4   THE SON-IN-LAW (1779)
- C5   FIRE AND WATER (1780)
- C6   THE WEDDING NIGHT (1780)
- C7   THE DEAD ALIVE (1781)
- C8   THE SILVER TANKARD or THE POINT AT PORTSMOUTH (1781)
- C9   HODGE-PODGE or A RECEIPT TO MAKE A BENEFIT (1781)
- C10 THE AGREEABLE SURPRISE or THE SECRET ENLARGED (1781)
- C11 NONE ARE SO BLIND AS THOSE WHO WON'T SEE (1782)
- C12 THE FEMALE DRAMATIST (1782)
- C13 THE BIRTH DAY or THE PRINCE OF ARRAGON (1783)
- C14 GRETNA GREEN (1783)
- C15 HUNT THE SLIPPER (1784)
- C16 PEEPING TOM (1784)
- C17 THE BASKET MAKER (1790)
- C18 THE CHILDREN IN THE WOOD (1793)
- C19 AULD ROBIN GRAY (1794)
- C20 RULE BRITANNIA! (1794)
- C21 BRITAIN'S GLORY or A TRIP TO PORTSMOUTH (1794)
- C22 THE DEATH OF CAPTAIN FAULKNOR or BRITISH HEROISM (1795)
- C23 WHO PAYS THE RECKONING? (1795)
- C24 LOVE AND MONEY or THE FAIR CALEDONIAN (1795)
- C25 BANNIAN DAY (1796)
- C26 THE SHIPWRECK (1796)
- C27 THE HOVEL (1797)
- C28 THE IRISH LEGACY (1797)
- C29 THROW PHYSICK TO THE DOGS or JACK OF ALL TRADES (1798)
- C30 THE REVIEW or THE WAGS OF WINDSOR (1800)
- C31 THE VETERAN TAR or A CHIP OF THE OLD BLOCK (1801)
- C32 THE SIXTY-THIRD LETTER or THE JOKE (1802)

D / Pasticcios and Other Operas with Contributions by Arnold

- D1   DAPHNE AND AMINTOR (1765)
- D2   THE SUMMER'S TALE (1765)
- D3   TOM JONES (1769)
- D4   AMINTAS (1769)
- D5   TRUE BLUE or THE PRESS GANG (1770)
- D6   THE SERAGLIO (1776)

D7	POLLY (1777)
D8	THE SHEEP-SHEARING (1777)
D9	A FAIRY TALE (1777)
D10	POOR VULCAN (1778)
D11	THOMAS AND SALLY or THE SAILOR'S RETURN (1794)
D12	VIRGINIA (1800)

E / *Pantomimes*

E1	HARLEQUIN DR. FAUSTUS (1766)
E2	THE RAPE OF PROSERPINE (1769)
E3	MOTHER SHIPTON (1770)
E4	THE GENIUS OF NONSENSE (1780)
E5	HARLEQUIN TEAGUE or THE GIANT'S CAUSEWAY (1782)
E6	HERE AND THERE AND EVERYWHERE (1785)
E7	THE GNOME or HARLEQUIN UNDERGROUND (1788)
E8	HARLEQUIN PEASANT or A PANTOMIME REHEARSED (1793)
E9	OBI or THREE FINGER'D JACK (1800)
E10	THE CORSAIR or THE ITALIAN NUPTIALS (1801)
E11	FAIRIES' REVELS or LOVE IN THE HIGHLANDS (1802)

F / *Incidental Music*

F1	MACBETH (1778)
F2	THE POSITIVE MAN (1782)
F3	FATAL CURIOSITY (1782)
F4	THE TOBACCO BOX or THE SOLDIER'S PLEDGE OF LOVE (1782)
F5	A BEGGAR ON HORSEBACK (1785)
F6	HOW TO BE HAPPY (1794)
F7	THE WEDDING DAY (1794)
F8	LOVE AND MADNESS! or THE TWO NOBLE KINSMEN (1795)
F9	OPHELIA'S SONGS IN *HAMLET* (1801?)

The Theater Music of Samuel Arnold:

A Thematic Index

Samuel Arnold in his doctoral robes

Engraving by Thomas Hardy, 1797.
Courtesy of the Trustees of the British Museum

INTRODUCTION

Arnold and the London Stage

Samuel Arnold (1740-1802) achieved his greatest heights as a dramatic composer who, besides pantomimes and incidental music, wrote, or contributed to, over seventy operas. The number of stage productions (and keyboard arrangements) of his theater works testifies to Arnold's popularity in the last quarter of the eighteenth century, and the statistical record of performances in *The London Stage*[1] shows that many of his operas were among the most frequently performed of the time. Arnold made his début at Covent Garden in 1765 with *The Maid of the Mill*, a full-scale pasticcio and a sampler of "action-finales" in English opera. Other early attempts in the field of dramatic music included writing all-sung burlettas for the outdoor theater at Marylebone Gardens. Beginning in 1777, Arnold mainly wrote "dialogue" operas for the Haymarket Little Theatre, which opened only during the summer period; this theater was successively under the management of George Colman, the elder (1732-94), and George Colman, the younger (1762-1836), who along with John O'Keeffe (1747-1833) were Arnold's chief librettists. Among the works that had the capacity to remain in the repertory were *The Spanish Barber* (1777), *The Son-in-Law* (1779), *The Agreeable Surprise* (1781), *The Castle of Andalusia* (1782), *Two to One* (1784), *Peeping Tom* (1784), *Inkle and Yarico* (1787), and *The Children in the Wood* (1793). No doubt the obvious charm and tunefulness of the music and the operatic comedy of the ensembles were largely responsible for this. During the 1790s Arnold wrote a series of experimental hybrid operas—plays for the chief characters but an opera for the subsidiary ones—set in the historic past. These works made greater use of chorus and instrumental numbers; they were in part a throwback to the musical episodes of the semi-operas of the seventeenth century and partly a desire to offer the public something more flexible than the usual comic opera of which it might be beginning to tire.

All-Sung Operas

Only two of Arnold's twelve listed all-sung operas were published; the rest, saving one single song, are lost. Considering the limited expectations of much of this repertory—six were written for the popular garden theater at Marylebone and two others were composed

---

[1] See *The London Stage 1660-1800*, vol. 5: *1776-1800*, ed. C. B. Hogan (Carbondale: Southern Illinois University Press, 1968).

John O'Keeffe, Irish dramatist, and librettist for some of Arnold's funniest operas

Engraving by Bragg, after a drawing
by Laurenson, 1786.
University of Oxford M.Adds.39.e.3.4.
Courtesy Bodleian Library

George Colman, the elder, who purchased the Haymarket Little Theatre in 1776 and promptly engaged Arnold as "house" composer

Oil painting by Thomas Gainsborough, ca. 1777.
Courtesy National Portrait Gallery

George Colman, the younger, who began to take over the Haymarket Little Theatre management from 1785; he was Arnold's most experimental librettist

Engraving by W. Greatbach, after De Wilde, 1837.
Courtesy Harvard Theater Collection, Houghton Library

The Haymarket Little Theatre and its successor, the New Haymarket Theatre, 1831

Courtesy Harvard Theater Collection, Houghton Library

The Haymarket Little Theatre in the 1790s

Courtesy Broadley Collection, City of Westminster Archives

INTRODUCTION

for specific occasions—and in the light of finding two listings unpopular, then questions of durability can be easily resolved. The two surviving scores, published in keyboard-vocal score, were *The Portrait* (**A6**) and *The Enraged Musician* (**A12**), successively Arnold's first and last collaboration with George Colman, the elder.

The Portrait stands squarely in the burletta tradition, recreating characters from the *commedia dell'arte*. The libretto is remarkable for the light bantering tone of the dialogue, and Colman's treatment of character and incident carries conviction. The symmetries of the plot are many: the first scene opens with Isabella gazing into a mirror, the second was Leander sighting Isabella, and the third with Pantaloon eyeing his painted portrait. In alliance with Arnold's music, the plot springs to palpitating life in the theater—especially in the quartet-finale when Pantaloon speaks from his own portrait, thereby confronting the young couple with their love-making; short-breathed responses build a flexible musical paragraph.

Ex. 1. *The Portrait*, no. 4, meas. 28-36.

The four characters in the opera are viewed symmetrically, two sentimental and two buffo. Isabella and Leander suffer the pangs of frustrated love, and as a consequence express a greater range of emotion. Isabella's coloratura in her second aria touches the springs of sensuality:

Ex. 2. *The Portrait*, no. 3, meas. 39-47.

The overture is suitably light-fingered, with a whiff of Arne's "Scotch Gavotte" movement from the overture to *Thomas and Sally* (1760) in the genial rondo.

The Enraged Musician, the last Arnold and elder Colman collaboration, apes the conventions and characters of contemporary opera. In the opening scene, Castruccio the music master sings, falsetto, "Non temer" from Bertoni's *Demofoonte*, an opera the success of which in 1778 was mainly due to the star castrato, Pacchierotti. His students, Piccolina and Castruccina, sing in turn a coloratura aria and a folksong, but Castruccio mistakes one for the other. Hogarth's painting, the springboard of the opera, is illustrated in the last scene. Castruccio, enraged that his daughter has eloped, leans out of the window to call for help; the din of the streetcriers exactly match his frantic expostulations:

Ex. 3. *The Enraged Musician*, no. 21, meas. 23-36.

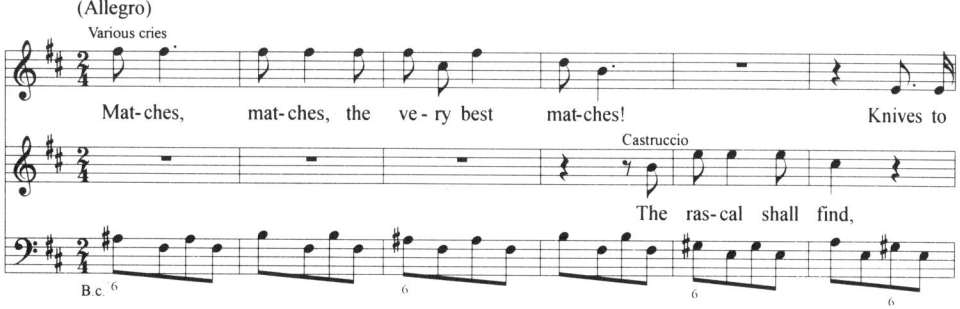

Continued

Ex. 3.—*Continued*

Mainpiece Operas with Spoken Dialogue

Seventeen of Arnold's eighteen mainpiece operas were published in keyboard-vocal score and circulated shortly after the first performance; none are preserved in manuscript. These three-act operas are in some ways his most ambitious works and they collectively constitute an important expression of the goals and values that formed the backbone of English comic opera. The effort of fuse stage action to music is well exhibited in the ensembles of the early- and middle-period operas and in the choral scenes of the later hybrids. The ensembles allow us to laugh at the characters' antics (we also feel for them), while the choral scenes galvanize turbulent passions. The range of emotion in Arnold's operas is widened by the treatment of heroines given long arias and coloratura; the music, in some respects the most memorable, explores the hair-line between comedy and tragedy. Brief tuneful songs are given to the lighter characters, though Arnold allows a more demanding level of singing for the maid who shares her mistress's thoughts. Folksong is employed most usefully to represent an earthy humanity; some of Arnold's English examples are previously unrecorded, while most of the Irish ones were sung to the composer by his Irish librettist John O'Keeffe.[2] The plan of Arnold's mainpiece operas generally includes a three-movement overture, about eighteen vocal numbers for the comic operas, and about eleven for the hybrids.

---

[2] O'Keeffe, *Recollections* (1826).

MAINPIECE OPERAS WITH SPOKEN DIALOGUE

The rustic setting of The Maid of the Mill, *as conceived by John Inigo Richards for the original production at Covent Garden, 31 January 1765*

Painting. Courtesy Paul Mellon Collection, Yale Center for British Art

Arnold became London's new theater composer with his setting of *The Maid of the Mill* (**B1**). The libretto, by Isaac Bickerstaffe (1733-1808?), is a sophisticated comedy with social overtones: Lord Aimworth, shrewd enough not to sacrifice love in order to satisfy the demands of one's social self, marries Patty, the miller's daughter.

> LORD AIMWORTH: I know very well the ridicule that may be thrown on a lord's marrying a miller's daughter; and I own the blushes, it has for some time had too great weight with me, but we should marry to please ourselves, not other people: and on mature consideration, I can see no reproach justly merited, by raising a deserving woman to a station she is capable of adorning, let her birth be what it will [3.xi.18-25].

9

Patty, modeled on Richardon's Pamela, became the prototype of the tender and loving young woman in English comic opera, and Arnold's judicious borrowing from Italian opera heightened her "emotional" presence. Arnold's new-composed ensembles give amplification, not just to the sentimental dimension of the plot but Bickerstaffe's timely social message as well. Thus, the finale to act 1 begins when Farmer Giles has just acquainted Patty with Lord Aimworth's seeming approval of their marriage. The music begins with Patty soliloquizing, but the entry of Giles and Patty's brother Ralph triggers comic stage movement:

Ex. 4. *The Maid of the Mill*, **B1.1**, meas. 1-17.

From *The Maid of the Mill* sprang a whole series of similar pastiche productions (some are discussed later), culminating in *The Castle of Andalusia* (**B5**), which proved to be one of the most popular operas of the period. John O'Keeffe's libretto with the castle, the forest, the cave-in-rock, the bandits, mistaken identities, and sudden recognitions, is very evidently a response to earlier Gothic fictions. The opera's romantic aspect is apparent in the opening scene, where the cave provides a backdrop for a chorus of robbers. The choral music is set in block harmony to give due reign to the lively orchestral writing, while the shadow of the hangman's noose is intensely observed in a central solo where the music moves through a sequence of minor keys. O'Keeffe introduces the topos of the secluded woman deprived of her property rights, and the heroine's viewpoint effects to energize Arnold's music. Victoria's G-major aria "Ah, Solitude take my distress," on the vicissitudes of love, is the most penetrating music in the opera. In the first part her

Title-page of The Castle of Andalusia
keyboard-vocal score, November 1782

Courtesy Royal College of Music, London

sighing phrases are associated with the solo flute, while the middle "D" section palpitating strings give a strong sense of her despair. At "each sigh" the music turns to a passage of searching progressions, which express well enough her seclusion:

Ex. 5. *The Castle of Andalusia*, **B5.6**, meas. 20-23.

Victoria's A-major aria "The musk rose" reverts to a lighter tone; the sequence of the opening melody leads to a tiny chromatic inflection, which is very effectively placed:

Ex. 6. *The Castle of Andalusia*, **B5.11**, meas. 14-18.

Act 1 is nearly all Arnold's own work, while the rest of the music chiefly makes use of Italian arias and British folksong. In his borrowings Arnold's almost invariable method was to employ an element of parody, drawing a parallel scene and situation to the original. Thus, when Alphonso sings "Love sweet poison," his farewell to Victoria (who has just married Fernando), to "Verdi prati" from Handel's *Alcina*, it is a readily understood cross-reference to Ruggiero's farewell to Alcina's enchanted island. In the original, Ruggiero's mood is a mixture of nostalgic regret and joy, and the same music serves to convey Alphonso's dual feelings of lamentation for the loss of Victoria, while at the same time looking to a joyous union with Lorenza.

After *The Castle of Andalusia*, Arnold and O'Keeffe wrote *The Siege of Curzola* (**B8**), first staged as a full-length opera but then reduced to an afterpiece. The score is remarkable in that it contains solos for three skilled sopranos—Elizabeth Bannister and Georgina George, the Haymarket Little Theatre's two best singers, and Giovanna Sestini, appearing as a guest from the King's Theatre. In Sestini's entrance aria "Sweet ladies," coloratura and reiterated trumpet-calls express resolution. The trio, in which the lovers sound in sweet thirds against Podesta's spouting semiquavers, is the opera's best comic moment.

Arnold's first major success at the Haymarket Little Theatre was *The Spanish Barber* (**B2**), a full-length opera based on the English version by Colman, the elder of Beaumarchais's *Le Barbier de Seville*.[3] The

Elizabeth Bannister, née *Harper, Arnold's star soprano at the Haymarket Little Theatre*

Engraving by J. Conde, 1793.
Courtesy Harvard Theater Collection, Houghton Library

---

[3] English translations and adaptations of Beaumarchais were quickly published (there had been an earlier one in 1776 by Elizabeth Griffiths), but not Colman's libretto, even though *The Spanish Barber* was popular for some twenty years. Colman's version left out the scene in which the Count plays his drunken soldier masquerade.

Ex. 7. *The Siege of Curzola*, no. 8, meas. 88-92.

published French text includes the vocal lines of two songs, of which the instantly popular "Je suis Lindor" was adopted by Arnold as Rosina's "Tell-tale eyes." The songs of Lazarillo (Figaro) express his exuberance with admirable energy, reinforced in his "barber" song by the illustrative orchestral details:

Ex. 8. *The Spanish Barber*, no. 4, meas. 10-32.

Continued

INTRODUCTION

Ex. 8.—*Continued*

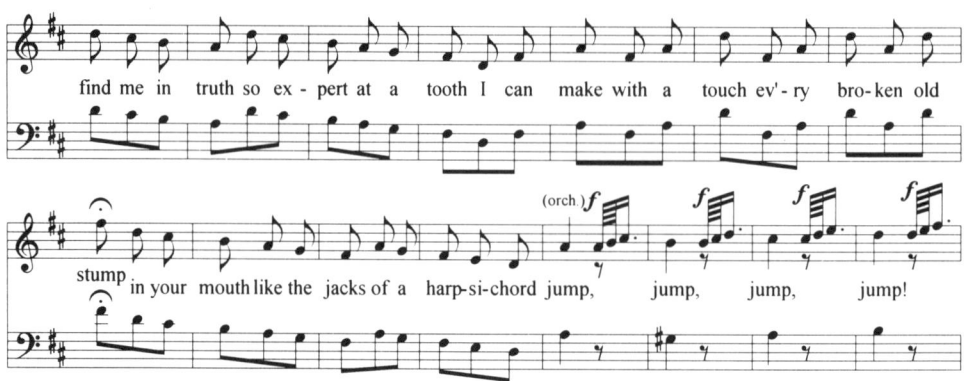

In contrast, Rosina's music is much more personal. Arnold employs G major, his favorite key for soliloquy, for her act 3 aria; the expressive flexibility of Arnold's melodic writing can be sampled in the opening:

Ex. 9. *The Spanish Barber*, no. 11, meas. 9-16.

During the music lesson Rosina sings "Love, the soul firing," and this modest song became the opera's most popular. Marked "Gayment," it was accompanied by some amusing stage action.

> While she is singing Bartolo falls asleep, which the Count observing, he and Rozina caress each other, and she leaves off at the word *gladness*—the orchestra then cease to play. As the noise of the musick has lulled the Doctor, the cessation of it arouses him, on which Rozina suddenly resumes the tune and finishes the air. Bartolo complains of modern tunes.[4]

---

[4] *Morning Chronicle*, 1 September 1777.

Arnold anticipated Paisiello's 1782 setting by giving Basil (Don Basilio), the music master, a long "rumor" aria with colorful invocations of musical instruments sounded in the accompaniment. The frantic expostulations, at once indignant and hilarious, strike the exact chord of impotent outrage. Especially funny is the trio-finale to act 1 between Bartholo and the two servants drugged by Lazarillo—one under the influence of a sleeping drug and the other of a sneezing powder; a sustained d' serves for yawning and octave leaps for the sneeze:

Ex. 10. *The Spanish Barber*, no. 6, meas. 81-89.

The single movement overture plays homage to the fandango theme in Gluck's *Don Juan* (1761), thereby suggesting the Spanish locale and perhaps romance in general:

Ex. 11. *The Spanish Barber*, overture, "El Fandango," meas. 1-6.

INTRODUCTION

Six of Arnold's full-length operas were set to libretti by George Colman, the younger. The earliest of these, *Two to One* (**B6**) and *Turk and No Turk* (**B7**), adopt the formula boy secretly courts girl, boy adopts disguise to win regard of girl's father (the obstacle of the course of true love), boy marries girl. From Arnold's music it is clear that the heroine is endowed with a wider range of emotion than everyone else. Charlotte's first aria in *Two to One* is another amorous pliant:

Ex. 12. *Two to One*, no. 1, meas. 12-20.

While it is in act 2 that she rises to her full stature:

Ex. 13. *Two to One*, no. 14, meas. 104-13.

One may note too that especially useful maids are also capable of expressing emotion, as Arnold shows by a touch here and there in the music for Fib in *Turk and No Turk*:

Ex. 14. *Turk and No Turk*, no. 2, meas. 53-62.

The overture to *Turk and No Turk* deserves mention as Arnold's best. The first movement, employing chromatic melodic material and some telling harmonic colorings, anticipates the arrival of the hero from Constantinople in his Turkish disguise. The richly expressed opening brings a foretaste of sentiment and also the idea of cultural collision, which furnishes the action to come:

Ex. 15. *Turk and No Turk*, overture, first movement, meas. 1-12.

In *Inkle and Yarico* (**B9**) Colman and Arnold tackle issues of gender and race in a manner at once comic and thought provoking. Much of the libretto goes into finding out the character of Inkle. Within minutes of landing in America he is calculating how many "natives cou'd be caught" and "how much they might fetch at the West India markets" (1.i.125-27), and within hours of his arrival he has been pursued by natives and saved by the protection of Yarico, who becomes his mistress. Inkle convinces Yarico to accompany him to the West Indies, where he has to decide between fidelity to her and a wealthy marriage to Narcissa, the governor's daughter; he chooses the money and offers to sell Yarico into slavery. It is this "barbarity" that provides most of the complications of the plot, with its climax in which Inkle faces the governor's questioning, is punished for his outlandish behavior, and marries Yarico, the girl who loves him. The hero of the subplot, Trudge, Inkle's servant, is the reverse of his master; he feels no inhibitions about loving Wowski, Yarico's maid. The audience laughs at his clownish ways, but his humanity exposes the whole sorry business of his master's avarice. What Colman does in marrying Inkle to Yarico is to make overt social/inter-racial connections where economic ones (during the era of plantations) already existed.

Arnold's music makes its most moving impression in the music for Yarico. When she sings of love she is very eloquent:

Ex. 16. *Inkle and Yarico*, no. 12, meas. 13-18.

We see Yarico from more than one angle, and her first solo befits her courage:

Ex. 17. *Inkle and Yarico*, no. 3, meas. 25-30.

Continued

Ex. 17.—*Continued*

Yarico wants her identity and her love for Inkle to merge, and the paradoxical result is that although she is betrayed by him she will not give him up because that would be to falsify herself.

On the other hand, Wowski and Trudge point directly at the presumed meaning of the opera; their innocent integrity indicates how imprisoned Inkle is in his motives:

Ex. 18. *Inkle and Yarico*, no. 6, meas. 15-19.

Playing on their English audience's investment in the idea of their own unsurpassed civilized state, Arnold and Colman ask them to prove themselves truly civilized by being civil to other races. *Inkle and Yarico* can also be read as issuing a challenge to the endogamy, which falsely represented the actual colonial ties producing English wealth (see illustration on following page).

History was a passion with Colman. He was addicted to Shakespeare's historical plays, which built up a vast picture in his mind of the men, women, and manners that had helped shape the destiny of England. His three historical hybrid productions—*The Battle of Hexham* (**B10**), *The Surrender of Calais* (**B12**), and *The Mountaineers* (**B14**)—reflected his

Libretto of Inkle and Yarico, *August 1787, with frontispiece showing Yarico "discover'd asleep" at the entrance of her cave; she is exotically dressed in skins and feathers*

University of Oxford, Vet A5.E.1150.
Courtesy Bodleian Library

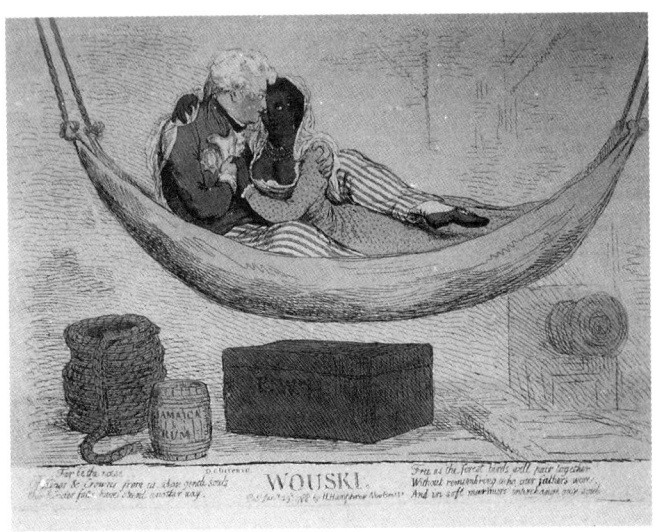

Cartoon depicting Prince William Henry as Trudge with Wowski in Inkle and Yarico

Engraving, 1788, by James Gillray.
Courtesy British Library

Sarah Harlowe as Adeline disguised as a soldier in The Battle of Hexham

Watercolor of W. Wellings, 1795.
Courtesy Garrick Club, London

interests and played to his strengths. Moreover, the play-opera structure of these works allowed Arnold to concentrate musically on the drama of Great Moments. In literary terms, Colman's historic dramas are too much imitative of Shakespeare's, but he possessed an individual sense of stagecraft and had an intuitive grasp of what pleases audiences: strong characters, even stronger situations, sharp attacks on the proprieties, and a capacity to surprise. John Genest was incensed by the "jumble of Tragedy, Comedy and Opera, with a ridiculous attempt at obsolete language,"[5] but he failed to recognize that the venture was a significant attempt to expand the formal limits of popular entertainment to include less easily digested material.

The characteristic tone of Arnold's music is inflatory, not only by virtue of the greater emphasis on chorus and orchestral marches but in its depiction of people of principle who rise up against tyranny to defend loyalty and right. The curtain of *The Battle of Hexham* rises on Adeline (see illustration above) as she goes in search of her husband, Gondibert, disguised as a soldier. In the opening, she unfolds strong impulses of feeling:

Ex. 19. *The Battle of Hexham*, no. 1, meas. 9-16.

Continued

---

[5] John Genest, *Some Account of the English Stage*, 10 vols. (Bath: Carrington, 1832), 7:40.

Ex. 19.—*Continued*

And so does Gondibert, alias the Robber Captain, who at every turn detects intrigues that spell danger to the throne of England. The orchestral opening of his long aria projects his resolute character:

Ex. 20. *The Battle of Hexham*, no. 9, meas. 5-11.

When the call comes, the chorus of soldiers ending act 1 unsheathe their swords to equip themselves heroically:

Ex. 21. *The Battle of Hexham*, no. 4, meas. 14-19.

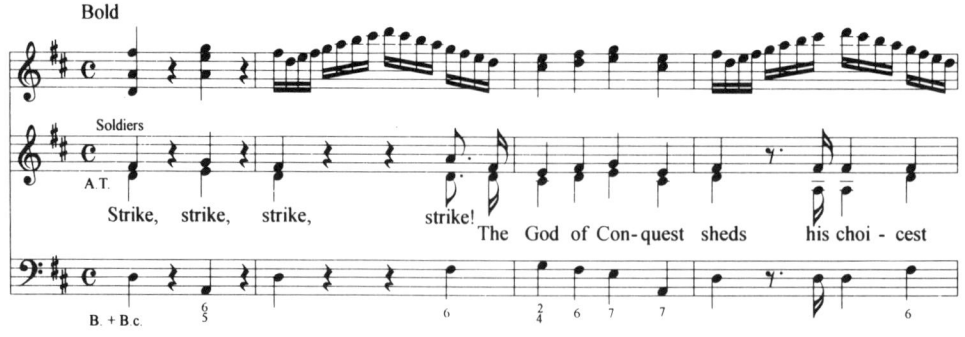

Continued

Ex. 21.—Continued

In *The Surrender of Calais*, an unusually chilly chorus of townsfolk intimates the execution of six innocent citizens in return for a general amnesty:

Ex. 22. *The Surrender of Calais*, no. 7, meas. 41-44.

This from a scene of the kind Colman's generation took to be "Shakespearean." And a Haydnesque trumpet signal with a roll of kettledrums opening the overture to *The Mountaineers* summons Zorayda in her plans to save Count Virolet, who has been jailed by the Moors:

Ex. 23. *The Mountaineers*, overture, first movement, meas. 1-9.

By far the most important from the point of view of music written in the last period of Arnold's operatic activity are the choruses, which attempt to evoke a picture of popular life. The basic idea of *Zorinski* (**B15**)—that of the patriotism of the Polish people—is introduced in the first chorus of peasants; Arnold's treatment is in alliance with Handel:

Ex. 24. *Zorinski*, no. 1, meas. 17-20.

There are also resonances of nationalism in the 3/4 polacca of the opening song; drumming bass notes suggest the drone of folk instruments:

Ex. 25. *Zorinski*, no. 2, meas. 9-12.

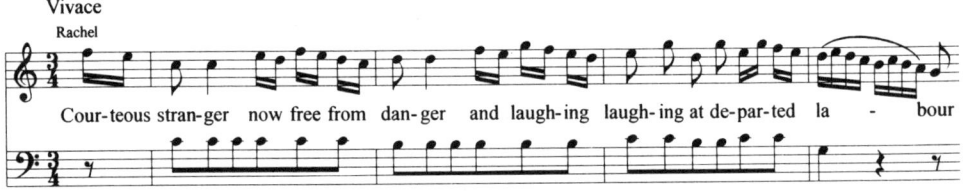

The use of pedal harps and union pipes in the overture to *Cambro-Britons* (**B17**) prepares the way for the chorus of Welsh bards, which gives powerful amplication to the culminating point of the action (ex. 26).

It is the overture to *The Enchanted Wood* (**B13**), a hybrid modeled on Shakespeare's *A Midsummer Night's Dream*, that strikes as the most remarkable stroke of the opera. The opening not only sounds entirely spontaneous but it also projects Mendelssohn's busy evocation of the fairy world (ex. 27). The second subject is a "reel" with drone D's, conjuring up the spell of the Scottish Highlands. The middle movement, a duet for horn and bassoon, anticipates a similar movement in the overture to *The Children in the Wood* (**C18**). In both these "woodland" operas the rondo finale theme reappears in the opera's final chorus.

Afterpiece Operas with Spoken Dialogue

Only half of the Arnold corpus of thirty-two afterpiece operas was printed, and no manuscript scores survive. In most cases the unprinted works met with little public success, while others were written for specific occasions with limited expectations of durability. The libretti of these works have mainly been preserved and some short songs were circulated in separate publications. Arnold's extant afterpieces were published in keyboard score: there are six with libretti by John O'Keeffe, three by the composer's son Samuel James Arnold, and one each by Colman (father and son), Henry Knapp, Thomas Morton,

Ex. 26. *Cambro-Britons*, no. 7, meas. 12-17.

Ex. 27. *The Enchanted Wood*, overture, first movement, meas. 1-6.

Robert Benson, George Brewer, and Wally Chamberlain Oulton. Arnold's approach to the afterpieces is akin to the generic comic opera style of the mainpieces with respect to song types, ensembles, and borrowings, but the composer's later hybridism is relatively unexplored. The shorter plan of the afterpiece generally favors a two-movement overture and ten to fifteen vocal numbers. Arias are linked with important singers and a central ensemble usually prescribes stage action. Arnold's collaborations with O'Keeffe, his son, and Morton (discussed below) are more carefully conceived than those with Brewer (**C25**), Colman, the younger (**C30**), and Oulton (**C32**). *Lilliput* (**C2**), *Hunt the Slipper* (**C15**), and *Love and Money* (**C24**) are small-scale scores: *Hunt the Slipper* and *Love and Money* contain some short songs and *Lilliput* is chiefly instrumental. The short overture for *Lilliput* cunningly identifies child actors representing Lilliputians by employing the nursery song "Boys and girls come out to play."

A comic but unnerving sense of displacement experienced by characters is perhaps the most important feature in the Arnold-O'Keeffe afterpieces. Moreover, individual insecurities seem to run counter to the general context, where part of the appeal is in the easy adjustment between characters and their environment. In *The Son-in-Law* (**C4**) the question of a father conferring a settlement on his unmarried daughter is adjourned in favor of the daughter's private needs; in the trio ending act 1, the parent sees there are two sides to every question, both of them reasonable:

Ex. 28. *The Son-in-Law*, no. 5, meas. 50-57.

The daughter's act 2 aria shows her seriously disturbed, and the shift from oboe and bassoon to violins orchestrally realizes the passion of her words:

Ex. 29. *The Son-in-Law*, no. 7, meas. 13-24.

O'Keeffe's use of uncertainties over inheritance in the plot of *The Dead Alive* (C7) presents some unsettling moments, especially when the dispossessed newlyweds, who fake each other's deaths to regain their inheritances, are rumbled by the elderly testators. The most striking part of Arnold's music is the presentation of the aged relatives at the point ending act 1 when they are pushed into action—with Sir Walter also taking a pot-shot at wooing Miss Hebe. Here, Sir Walter's advances are left looking rather wan in the light of Miss Hebe's fierce reaction; Arnold sums up the impact in a change of rhythm and a sequential climb back to the tonic D:

Ex. 30. *The Dead Alive*, no. 7, meas. 31-50.

What is clearly under some scrutiny in *The Agreeable Surprise* (**C10**) is the question of misalliance. Laura's courtship with Eugene is theoretically a misalliance, but it is all right in the end because of the money he brings, her virtue, and because the love between them is the real thing. The obstinacy of Sir Felix Friendly in waiting to reveal to the lovers their bizarre history (they are swapped at birth) is inextricably bound up with the soft-heartedness that loves to "surprise people with good news" (1.i.83-84)—so his intransigence becomes the register of his humanity. The opera's energies derive from the benign presence of rustic life, sounded first in the *siciliana* accents of the overture:

Ex. 31. *The Agreeable Surprise*, overture, first movement, meas. 1-4.

A jolly chorus of harvesters follows, and then a variety of short songs representing country characters. Laura's vocal virtuosity precisely illustrates her ardent mood in the G-major "lark" aria, in which voice and obbligato flute alternatively climb and fall to trace the bird's flight; at this point both soloists achieve unclouded happiness:

Ex. 32. *The Agreeable Surprise*, no. 5, meas. 41-52.

INTRODUCTION

The first act finale starts out on a characteristic trajectory from stasis (preparations for the wedding) to surprise (Sir Felix's unwelcome announcement of the husband for Laura) and distress (the lovers stumped). In this section the dispirited sweethearts blend in honeyed thirds while Sir Felix cheerfully orders wine to celebrate:

Ex. 33. *The Agreeable Surprise*, no. 7, meas. 54-76.

The opera chiefly owed its popularity to the novelty of the acting, especially that of John Edwin as Lingo, the verbose schoolmaster-turned-butler who is continually spouting favorite Latin tags. Lingo's "Amos, amas, I love a lass," sung to Cowslip the dairymaid (see illustration on opposite page), became the opera's hit success; the borrowed tune, a meaningfully conveyed parody, is "The mouse and the frog" ("A frog he would a'wooing go").

30

John Edwin as Lingo the schoolmaster-butler woos Mary Wells as Cowslip the dairymaid in The Agreeable Surprise

Drawing by John Downman, 1787.
Courtesy Paul Mellon Collection, Yale Center for British Art

INTRODUCTION

Arnold's music for *The Birth Day* (**C13**) and *Gretna Green* (**C14**; song-words by O'Keeffe) is narrower in compass, but a "sea-battle" aria in *Gretna Green* is well contrived from the pictorial angle to make a stunning effect in the theater:

Ex. 34. *Gretna Green*, no. 14, meas. 66-99.

Ex. 34.—*Continued*

In *Peeping Tom* (**C16**), the last of their extant afterpieces, Arnold emerges with more credit than O'Keeffe. His scoring shows how much variety was possible with the limited resources of the Little Theatre band (see illustration on following page), and he sets some previously unrecorded English folksongs—for example, "We go up Holborn Hill," sung while the Mayor of Coventry makes advances to Peeping Tom's wife:

Ex. 35. *Peeping Tom*, no. 3 (complete tune).

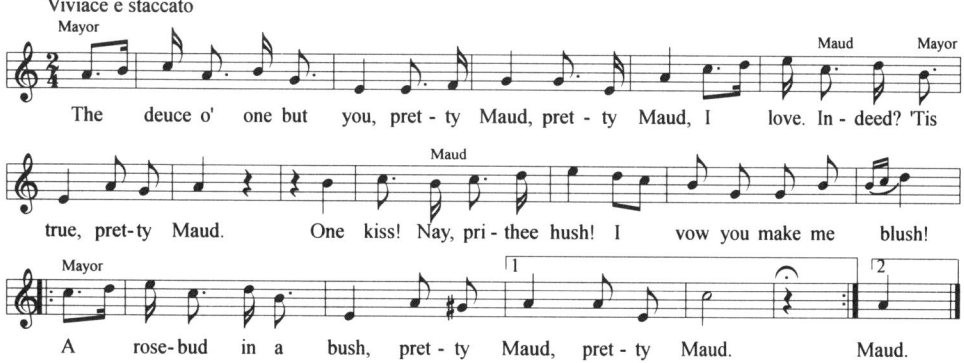

Unfortunately, too many episodes in the libretto that demand music—when the Mayor hides in a basket and when Tom is caught peeping at Lady Godiva—receive none, and this failure has a leaden effect.

Page from Harrison's keyboard-vocal score of Peeping Tom *(second movement of the overture), showing a rich variety of orchestral cues*

University of Oxford, Harding Mus.D.40.
Courtesy Bodleian Library

Arnold's *The Children in the Wood* (**C18**) became one of the most popular afterpiece operas of the 1790s and enjoyed prolonged success both in England and America throughout the first decades of the nineteenth century.[6] The libretto, by Thomas Morton (1764-1838), is a skillfully fleshed-out version of "The Babes in the Wood" with a happy ending. John Bannister became famous for his role as Walter,[7] the woodcutter who rescues the children. The *London Chronicle*, 1-3 October 1793, noted that Bannister's performance was an "exquisite delineation of the mixed emotions of Pity, Love, Terror, Transport, and Despair. . . . Nothing could be more rapturous than his interview with the infants after their recovery. Nothing more perfectly true to nature, than his agitation in the scene where Mrs. Bland sings the old ballad ["The Ditty"] with a captivation that subdues every heart."

---

[6] For American alterations, see Susan L. Porter's introduction (pp. xvii-xviii) to *The Children in the Wood*, referenced under **C18**. See also her "Children in the Wood: The Odyssey of an Anglo-American Ballad," in *Vistas of American Music: Essays and Compositions in Honor of William K. Kearns*, ed. Porter and John Graziano (this publisher, 1998).

[7] See John Adolphus, *Memoirs of John Bannister*, 2 vols. (London: Bentley, 1839), 1:316-21.

Arnold's score is, in its modest way, a little masterpiece, with the flickering emotional cross-currents between tragedy and farce, irony and pathos, held artfully in balance. Not its least remarkable feature is the overture in which Arnold is careful to touch in the shadows. Beginning in the tonic D minor, at first in octaves, the music leads via the dominant to a D-major Allegro and apparently standard first-movement form. After the development, however, there is a dominant preparation that seems to signal the recapitulation but instead introduces a lyric slow movement, the calm of which is touchingly expressive as a consequence. The central movement is based on the tune known as "Three children sliding on the ice,"[8] a cross-reference warning to the children, sounded by the horns followed by solo violin. The second movement leads without a break into a brisk trumpet rondo, with a "Turkish" march in the "B" section, illustrating the hired assassins. A duple version of the ballad melody returns as a finale episode. The trumpet rondo recurs in the opera's final chorus.

The little girl's song, sung in the wood to comfort her brother (see illustration), brings out their vulnerability. Arnold uses a flageolet to represent the robin's song, and this independent line makes graceful play over the pulsating strings. The music looks simple enough on paper but it exactly matches the affecting scene (ex. 36).

Frederick and Mary Menage sing the "bird" duet in the original production of The Children in the Wood

Engraving by Barlow, after Cruikshank, 1793.
Courtesy Harvard Theater Collection, Houghton Library

Josephine's sad song, sung in the forest hut at night, is actually a folksong called "The Norfolk Tragedy" in the libretto and "The Ditty" by Arnold (see illustration on following page). It is a version of the Herefordshire folk-carol published subsequently by Vaughan Williams as "The Truth from Above," but Arnold's source is not known; he appears to have deliberately introduced sharpened sixths and sevenths into an otherwise modal tune (ex. 37).

---

[8] Also as "Now ponder well, ye parents dear"; see no. 12 of *The Beggar's Opera*.

Ex. 36. *The Children in the Wood*, no. 5, meas. 18-25.

The Children in the Wood, *John Bannister as Walter agitated by Josephine's sad song "The Norfolk Tragedy," or "The Ditty" as Arnold called it*

Oil on canvas by Samuel Dehilde.
Courtesy Somerset Maugham Collection,
Royal National Theatre, London

Ex. 37. *The Children in the Wood*, no. 8 (complete tune).

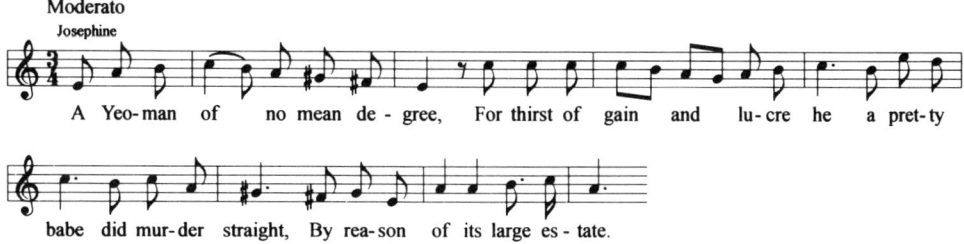

The farcical "supper" ensemble ending act 1 allows full freedom of stage movement. In this passage the maid avoids the indignities of the old uncle's advances while the butler recites the menu; the uncle doesn't sing, but the vigorous orchestra comically illustrates what he is up to:

Ex. 38. *The Children in the Wood*, no. 4, meas. 1-14.

Auld Robin Gray (**C19**), set in the Scottish Highlands, is the first of three extant operas set to libretti by the composer's son Samuel James Arnold.[9] The employment of authentic folk music is widespread in the score and complemented by Arnold writing his own music in the Scottish style, as for the reunited lovers here:

---

[9] Samuel James Arnold (1774-1852), librettist (30 stage works) and impresario. In 1815 he rebuilt the Lyceum Theatre as the English Opera House; his production of Weber's *Der Freischütz* (1824) was the first in England. Arnold was also a skilled artist (see illustrations, pp. xix, 40).

Ex. 39. *Auld Robin Gray*, no. 13, meas. 17-28.

The second Arnold father-son opera is their best. *The Shipwreck* (**C26**), a tale of smuggling set among the cliffs of Cornwall, begins dramatically with a storm overture, which continues to rage under much of the opening chorus:

Ex. 40. *The Shipwreck*, no. 1, meas. 26-39.

Ex. 40.—*Continued*

the foam - ing sur - ges break, that
the foam - ing sur - ges break, that
the foam - ing sur - ges break, that
lash, that lash the shore; that lash, that lash the shore
lash, that lash the shore; that lash, that lash the shore
lash, that lash the shore; that lash, that lash the shore

Another memorable moment is associated with Angelica in the E♭-major aria sung as she scans the sea for her lost lover; the ritornello previews her sighs:

Ex. 41. *The Shipwreck*, no. 2, meas. 1-10.

Andante
Oboe
[f]
V. I, II
[p]
Bassoon

Continued

Ex. 41.—*Continued*

Unfortunately, Arnold's libretto does not allow the outcome of the conflict between smugglers and those shipwrecked to be resolved. Apart from the coastal scene, the one episode enabling the composer to build up dramatic tension is the quartet in which knocking at the door startles the smugglers as they stash their treasure; before the end, *pizzicato* strings in unison represent a nocturnal striking of the village clock. More sea music was written for *The Veteran Tar* (**C31**), but nothing up to the standard of *The Shipwreck*.

Title-page of The Shipwreck, *after Samuel James Arnold?, showing exterior sets of the seacoast and the smuggler's pub*

Engraving by Thomas King, 1796.
University of Oxford, Mus.I.100(10). Courtesy Bodleian Library

Pasticcios and Other Operas with Contributions by Arnold

Of the twelve works listed in this category, four (**D1-D4**) are pasticcios, two are completions of operas by Charles Dibdin (**D6, D10**), two are musical settings for the elder Colman's Shakespeare adaptations (**D8-D9**), two are revivals (**D5, D11**), one is a ballad opera (**D7**), and another is an arrangement of accompaniments (**D12**). The extent of Arnold's involvement with the four pasticcio operas is not always clear, but he sometimes seems to have shared the arranging with other composers. The music to be singled out in the pasticcios is Arnold's aria for Amelia in *The Summer's Tale* (**D2**), when she drops the disguise of a madwoman to run into Frederick's arms; breathless Purcellian sobs in C minor break into E♭ and a "trumpet-tune" flourish to signify her joy:

Ex. 42. *The Summer's Tale*, **D2.6**, meas. 61-69.

Arnold's music for *The Seraglio* (**D6**) and *Poor Vulcan* (**D10**) is marked by his desire to blend in with Dibdin's own style. For example, **D6.1** is a direct imitation of Mungo's song in *The Padlock*.

Ex. 43a. *The Seraglio*, **D6.1**, meas. 46-56.

Continued

Ex. 43a.—*Continued*

Ex. 43b. Charles Dibdin, *The Padlock* (London: author, [1768]), p. 18, meas. 1-8.

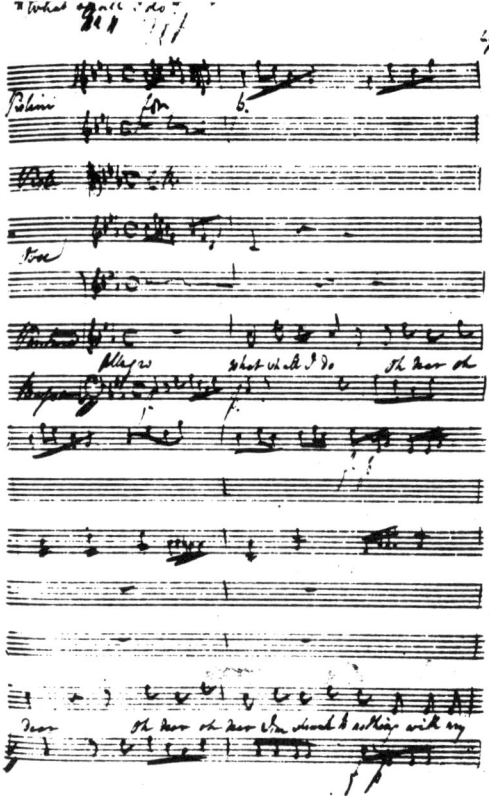

Arnold's autograph manuscript of the beginning of Venture's song (first version) for Dibdin's The Seraglio, *1776*

Courtesy British Library

Whereas the Colman Shakespeare settings are lost, Arnold's music for Colman's cut version of John Gay's *Polly* (**D7**) survives in orchestral parts. In *The Beggar's Opera*, Gay exposed the darker side of society that undercut the surface glitter of the age, while in the sequel *Polly* the heroine finally rejects the values of her materialistic society to live apart from other whites, sharing the life of the wilderness with her Indian husband, Cawwawkee. Arnold's newly-composed music focuses upon two elements of the drama—the identification of war or warlike acts of violence as the agent of progress, and political reconciliation mirrored in the romantic alliance between hero and heroine representing different cultures. The medley overture of tunes culled from *The Beggar's Opera*[10] cunningly recovers the heroine's past, while the central suite-like dance of pirates (including two hornpipes) represents the crisis of social and ideological conflicts. The group of Indian dances show in the resolution a definite step towards reconciliation; here, the double stopping, made to sound exotic, celebrates the quest for spiritual renewal in a savage wilderness:

Ex. 44. *Polly*, D7.19e, meas. 1-4.

It is not difficult to locate plot action in the ballet music. The flourish of sixteenth notes in the final pirate dance, for example, seems to signal the capture of Cawwawkee:

Ex. 45. *Polly*, D7.6e, meas. 1-4.

---

[10] If an overture by Pepusch existed, it is lost.

INTRODUCTION

Hester Colles in the title role of Polly; *she sang "horribly out of tune"*

Colored drawing by J. Roberts, 1778.
Courtesy British Library

And the lyricism of the fourth Indian dance suggests this is likely the moment when Polly makes her vows to Cawwawkee:

Ex. 46. *Polly*, **D7.19d**, meas. 1-4.

Arnold acknowledges Polly as protagonist in music, which shows a capacity for action as well as tenderness. Her entrance solo begins with a sighing motive which is reserved for her throughout:

Ex. 47. *Polly*, **D7.2**, meas. 9-16.

In his borrowings, Arnold creates additional openings for ironic cross-reference—for example, Polly's lament for the pirate Morano (Macheath) is set to Arne's pungent music for Abel's death in the oratorio *The Death of Abel* (1744). Since Arne's aria does not otherwise survive, we cannot judge how his scoring may have compared with Arnold's:

Ex. 48. *Polly*, act 3, no. 6, meas. 9-12.

INTRODUCTION

Pantomimes

Eleven pantomimes by Samuel Arnold are listed. Although most of these works (**E1-E8**) belong to the Harlequin-athlete-trickster tradition, his three, and final, dramatic pantomimes (**E9-E11**) reveal the influence of early Romanticism. Of the Harlequin inspired works, the first four (excluding **E2**, for which Arnold wrote additional music) were published. The popularity of **E1** can be judged from the fact that it was the very first pantomime to be printed complete in a keyboard-vocal score format. The vogue for Harlequin pantomime seems on the decline by the mid-1780s; neither the scores nor the song-words of **E6-E8** was published. The Harlequin plot lines contain some elements which we think of as folk-tale motives: that of the magic token, the magic flight (escaping from a pursuer by means of magically interposed obstacles), the helpful genii or dwarf, the cruel sorcerer, the hero outwitting the stupid ogre, and the comic motives such as the two-headed giant or the goblet of wine that empties itself. Satire is also evident in the ridicule aimed at medical practices of the time[11] and theatrical affairs.[12]

The Harlequin scores by Arnold are largely composed of binary character or action pieces. These short instrumental movements are usually given titles to identify staging. Indeed, even without an extant libretto, it is easy to locate the main actions of the story. In *Harlequin Dr. Faustus* (**E1**), for example, falling eighth-note figures depict the Miller sobbing when Harlequin Faustus brings on a crisis (no. 8), and a violent Allegro with thrusting figuration signals the arrival of the Furies (no. 4). A feature of the dressing-room episode is a clock ticking *pizzicato* eighth notes (no. 18), and rolling figuration represents a rural scene with a mill (no. 21). In *Mother Shipton* (**E3**) there are pieces called "Tower scene" (no. 8), "Thames" (no. 9), and "Cornhill" (no. 12), and no doubt the audience witnessed figures running against a backdrop depicting these familiar places. Other events take place in the countryside, and Arnold usually peppers the music with Scotch-snap rhythms. The music for the coal-pit, near Mother Shipton's cave, explores some sort of linkage between dramatic and tonal tension:

Ex. 49. *Mother Shipton*, no. 24, complete.

---

[11] Especially those of James Graham's electrical treatments (**E4**) and Gustavus Katterfelto's "solar microscope" (**E5**; also **C11**); see illustration on opposite page.

[12] Including sly references to actor-managers David Garrick (**E1**) and Richard Brinsley Sheridan (**E8**).

Ex. 49.—*Continued*

In *The Genius of Nonsense* (**E4**) a bedroom minuet with two trios (no. 5) is followed by a fearful scurrying in sixteenth notes when Pantaloon chases after Harlequin (no. 6). An episode at Westminster Abbey begins with scales pealing bells (no. 9), while a dirge-like no. 10 in E♭ major represents the tombs; Harlequin expresses sorrowful sentiments in G-minor music with drooping sighs (no. 11). *Harlequin Teague* (**E5**) begins dramatically with the onset of a storm, but farce soon prevails. A splendidly raucous scene depicts Pierrot sleeping to a soothing lullaby (no. 24), which also includes "tiptoe" music as Harlequin enters the room holding a dark lantern. Thrusting music ensues with syncopated upward leaps as Harlequin stuffs a pillow over Pierrot's head and runs off with Columbine (nos. 24-25).[13]

James Graham and Gustavus Katterfelto,
whose cure-alls touch the buffoonery in The Genius of Nonsense, *1780,*
and None Are So Blind as Those Who Won't See, *1782*

Caricature by an unknown engraver.
Courtesy British Library

---

[13] Described in the *Morning Herald*, 19 August 1782.

On average, the vocal music occupies less than a quarter of the Harlequin scores (but in **E4** almost half). Most frequently, commonplace characters (rustics, sailors, publicans) are associated with cheerful ballad-style songs, while those with powerful influence (Helen of Troy in **E1**, Mother Shipton in **E3**, Genius of Ireland in **E5**) have music generally more diverse in character and employ coloratura. Full of humor is the "medical catch" in **E4**, where the distraught patients approach the doctor; a conflation of actions probably corresponded to the music and Arnold cannily slips to the dominant when the cure is announced:

Ex. 50. *The Genius of Nonsense*, no. 21, meas. 31-35.

The dramatic pantomimes, **E9-E11**, are generally much longer than the Harlequin ones, and their entire emphasis is on romantic action. In all these the story was mimed by actors to continuous orchestral music and with occasional vocal numbers interspersed. In addition, each was set in an exotic locale and included supernatural events, spectacular effects, processions, combat, and rescue. The ambitious dramatic scale of these theater pieces admitted many possibilities in script and staging, and Arnold was even more compelled than previously to make extensive musical cross-references between the use of mime and its integration into musical numbers. The use of such terms as "Grand Pantomimical Drama," "Grand Romantick Ballet," and "A Story told by Action interspersed with Songs, Recitative etc." to describe the provenance or genre shows clearly the attempt to convey the difference between these and hybrid stage works which had been popular hitherto.

Obi: or, Three Finger'd Jack (**E9**) is loosely based upon the Jamaican stories of Jack Mansong, a Negro outlaw driven by the realities of slavery to react violently. The shadowy hero, with his severed hand (hence the nickname) and uncanny powers of sorcery (*obeah*) leads in a series of raids on the English plantation. In his libretto John Fawcett introduces Rosa and Captain Orford as hero and heroine and the saga of their imprisonment in Jack's cave.

In his score Arnold seems to have made the crucial discovery that form can be translated according to dramatic situation.[14] A striking example is the Rondo Andante portraying Rosa. The graceful shape of the G-major rondo theme with flute obbligato projects the picture of Rosa as she begins to distribute gifts to the slave community on her birthday:

Ex. 51. *Obi*, no. 8, meas. 1-11.

The first episode, for strings, represents Rosa meeting Orford; the tonality shifts to the sharp side to show her reaction:

Ex. 52. *Obi*, no. 8 (cont.), meas. 14-17.

---

[14] For a full discussion of the music and also racial issues, see the *Music for London Entertainment* edition of *Obi* cited in **E9**.

*Maria DeCamp as Rosa sings a "Spanish" guitar-song to
Charles Kemble as Jack, act 2,* Obi: or, Three-Finger'd Jack

Engraving by Orme, after a watercolor by Harrison, 1800.
Courtesy Harvard Theater Collection, Houghton Library

The decisive music of the second episode sounds like Orford's signal back to camp and suggests gestures of frustration. The final reprise of the rondo theme returns Rosa to her original softened mood, now emerging from love.

Another example of Arnold's ability to match dramatic event with musical gesture is the first half of the scene inside Jack's cave. It opens with a lengthy Andante that accompanies the movement of Jack and Rosa about the cave, and closes with Jack singing what could be a charm (the words pseudo-Jamaican or African), then requesting Rosa to sing a song. Her response, a "Spanish" lullaby accompanied by *pizzicato* strings to suggest the sound of a guitar, is one of the high points of the pantomime (see illustration above); Jack evidently falls asleep during the course of the song. The Andante that follows (in an abrupt modulation to D major from the song's B♭) illustrates how closely Arnold's music at times appears to correspond to stage action. Rosa seems to have been moving stealthily about the cave during the six measures following the end of her song when she hears a groan, represented in a pungent falling semitone; a reprise of the quick note "tiptoe" music suggests more movement which is cut short, perhaps indicating that Jack has stirred in his sleep. Rosa repeats the last two lines of her song, possibly to quiet Jack.

Ex. 53. *Obi*, no. 46, complete.

Following this is heard a 16-measure development of the Andante theme, then 11 measures of new material, plus 8 measures of the initial Andante and 8 of the new material. Presumably Rosa here explores the cave, finds the prisoner's cell, opens the door, and discovers her wounded lover. The unsettled harmonies closing the passage may signal the moment when Orford is discovered.

Most of *Obi*'s score is by Arnold, yet there are some curious but effective borrowings, including the "Surprise" movement of Haydn and the Andante of Mozart's String Quartet in D, K. 575. The "Surprise" music accompanies a "magic" ceremony, and Mozart's quartet movement represents the entry of the wounded Orford after Jack's first attack. Haydn's music remains unchanged, but Mozart's is freely adapted into the sequence of measures 1-15, 19-29, 40-42, and 9-19, this constituting somewhat less than two-thirds of the original. Here, for example, are measures 13-15 and 19-23 of Arnold's first dovetailing:

INTRODUCTION

Ex. 54. *Obi*, no. 12, Andante, meas. 13-20.

Especially since Mozart's chamber music was little known in late eighteenth-century London, this adaptation may well have been the first public performance of this work in England (the score had been imported by Longman & Broderip after 1791).

The Corsair: or, The Italian Nuptuals (**E10**) is Arnold's most melodramatic pantomime. Set against a background of castles, rugged coasts, and the eruption of Mount Vesuvius (musically depicted in scale runs), the heroine Fiorita is kidnapped on her wedding day by the tyrannous pirate Tomar; Gagliardo follows his quest for love and his bride. Breakneck pursuits alternate with scenes of passionate feeling to forge a mixture of the psychology of terror and poetic description that belongs to the Gothic fantasies of the Romantics. Rescue finally comes when Fiorita's murdered father appears as an agent of retribution; gong strokes represent his arrival. Tomar fires his pistol at the ghost and the castle itself crumbles to the ground:

Ex. 55. *The Corsair*, no. 50, meas. 22-47; no. 51, meas. 1-4.

Ex. 55.—*Continued*

With respect to Arnold's later pantomimes, *Fairies' Revels: or, Love in the Highlands* (**E11**) is conspicuous for the folk element and also music for dance. Set in the Scottish Highlands, Donald, a young clansman, falls in love with Isabel and encounters a whole cast of fairies and other supernatural effects; he wins his bride and the recognition of Isabel's suspicious old father. The courting rituals, the fairyland hallucination, and the forest imbroglio are reminiscent of Shakespeare's *A Midsummer Night's Dream*. Arnold employs "Blue bells of Scotland" as a point of lyrical expression in the course of the overture and again when Isabel dances for Donald; his arrangement opens with two cellos alone:

Ex. 56. *Fairies' Revels*, no. 12 (= overture, second movement), meas. 1-8.

Incidental Music

Arnold wrote incidental songs for various plays, one each for **F2**, **F3**, **F5**, and **F7**, five for **F6**, and six for **F8**. Of these, only one of the five songs composed for **F6** seems to have survived, and the settings for **F8** are lost. The extant songs are all in ballad style, and Maria's tragic "Cease, cease, heart-easing tears" in *Fatal Curiosity* (**F3**) is sung on stage as a folk ballad. *The Tobacco Box* (**F4**), for two voices, takes the form of a dialogue-ballad, though its classification as an incidental interlude likens it to a serenata. For Hermia's mad-songs in *Love and Madness* (**F8**) Arnold may have adopted known theater tunes; those for Ophelia in **F9** are certainly traditional.

Arnold's incidental music for *Macbeth* (**F1**) serves to give a view of the action, expressing what has happened and to show it in perspective. The opening "March for *Macbeth*" is a symbol of the battle Shakespeare describes and of Macbeth's part therein. On the other hand, the "Menuetto to be play'd at the banquet" (act 3, scene 4), in D major and quasi-Scots style, signals the feast as a symbol of order. Arnold is sensitive to the meaning of source texts in the Scots songs he employs for several numbers. "The birks of Invermay," a song based on the idea that Time erodes, is placed early to point out that Macbeth's good beginning somehow leaves the future open and ambiguous, and "The Earl of Douglas's lament," a chivalrous song of piety and farewell, adds a further strand to Macduff's reaction to Ross's bitter news (act 4, scene 3). The "lament" music, with Arnold's rich, dark scoring, becomes a prayer of anguish:[15]

Ex. 57. *Macbeth*, **F1.7**, meas. 1-8.

---

[15] If one wanted to stage *Macbeth* with Arnold's music, another item could be included, namely "Duncan's Warning" (composed 1801; autograph in the Royal College of Music, Ms. 15, ff. 49-52b), an AATB glee in the composer's "romantic" style where tonal action matches the acceleration of changes; this piece would make a natural introduction to act 1, scene 6.

Conclusion

Arnold's theater music was influential on the London stage in the late eighteenth century, and the study of his wide range of works illuminates our understanding of the English comic opera subgenera. Furthermore, the melodramatic and sentimental features of the composer's dramatic style receive in his best work memorably explicit treatment. Concomitant with these features, it seems, is a congeries of specifically defined attitudes, some of which are shown to be challenging as well as funny: women are superior to men (confirmed in soliloquy arias with ornamental vocal lines); children are wiser than parents (pompous or touchy music associated with the "parent" operates as a limiting factor); emotions are less fallible than reason (sensuous aria settings, touching sadness tinged with passion, inherit the width of Arnold's sympathies); the lower classes are upgraded (displayed in an expressive use of folksong); the past is better than the present (ceremonial choruses act as a source of strength). If ordinary demotic sentimentality turns Arnold and his librettists into propagandists for humanitarian causes, then the mass sentimentality in response to, say, *Inkle and Yarico*, may have served to abolish slavery; or the affliction of the youngsters in *The Children in the Wood* to outlaw child labor.

The study of Arnold offers new perspectives on the work of a composer writing for an unassuming audience in a small London theater. The technique of most of Arnold's singers was very modest: only Elizabeth Bannister (Harper), and to a lesser degree Georgina George, had any claims to be singers of the first rank. The limited capacity of the Little Theatre company is obvious from an inspection of Arnold scores, yet it manages to operate not as a limiting factor but as a source of strength, especially in characterization. An inspired economy likewise distinguishes Arnold's scoring, almost exclusively of flutes or oboes, bassoons, horns, strings, and continuo, with trumpets and drums reserved for ceremonial moments. Many of the big arias achieve striking effects by the use of solo woodwind with an expanded string layout. Otherwise there are picturesque touches in the use of flageolet, piccolo, fife, harps, union pipes, clarinet, contrabassoon, gong, and keyboard glockenspiel. Arnold possessed the faculty not only for discovering the most suitable material within his resources, but for doing so at the right time.

A Thematic Index*

A / All-Sung Operas

A1 **ROSAMOND**
Opera in 1 act; music mostly not extant
Librettist unknown (after Joseph Addison's libretto)
First performed at Covent Garden, 21 April 1767

A1.1 Song: Eleanor

A1.1 (act 2) is the only number to survive; there are several copies of it (RISM A2426-31). It was printed by P. W[elcker] (ca. 1770) in score (two flutes, two bassoons, and strings). William Ayrton, *The Harmonicon* 8 (1830): 137, mentions the popularity of this song. Fiske, *Theatre Music*, 318, suggests that the libretto about the tragic consequences of sexual jealousy, was the same one Thomas Arne used in his afterpiece version of Addison's text (1740). According to Busby, *Anecdotes*, 3:54, this resetting was inferior to Arne's. There was only one performance. A copy of the printed libretto (London: L. Davis and C. Reymers, 1767) is in the Bodleian Library: Vet.A5e.2844; libretto reveals recitatives, 19 vocal numbers lost; also overture.

A2 **THE ROYAL GARLAND**
Occasional interlude in 1 act; music not extant
Libretto by Isaac Bickerstaffe
First performed at Covent Garden, 10 October 1768

This work, cast in the form of an allegorical pastoral, was written to celebrate the royal visit of Christian VII of Denmark. The *Public Advertiser* of 11 October 1768 reports that the music gave "general satisfaction." A copy of the printed libretto (London: T. Becket and P. A. de Hondt) is in the British Library: 161.e.28; Larpent Ms. 286. Printed libretto reveals recitatives, "Garland Dance," 8 vocal numbers, lost; also overture.

---

* Major keys are uppercase (A = A major); minor keys are lowercase (a = A minor).

A Thematic Index

A3 **THE SERVANT MISTRESS**
Burletta in 2 acts; Arnold's music not extant
Libretto by Stephen Storace, the elder, and John Trusler (adaptation of Gennaro Federico's *La serva padrona*, 1733)
First performed at Marylebone Gardens, 16 June 1770

This version of Giovanni Pergolesi's opera, including "Alterations and additional Songs" by Arnold (*Public Advertiser*, 16 June 1770), was later adapted by John O'Keeffe to make *The Maid's the Mistress* (Covent Garden, 14 February 1783).

A4 **THE REVENGE**

Arnold has been credited with the composition of the music for this burletta, which Thomas Chatterton wrote for Marylebone Gardens. However, the case is largely circumstantial as Arnold indicates in a letter to T. Park dated 24 February 1799 and printed in the *Monthly Mirror* 16 (September 1803): 168: "Dr Arnold . . . remembers Mr. Atterbury's giving five guineas to the late Mr. Chatterton, for some verses or poems . . . and that he saw the book which contained them at Teddington about five years ago. If the book contained a burletta called 'The Revenge,' it *never was performed* at Marylebone Gardens." A song Chatterton wrote for *The Revenge* ("Away to the woodlands") was published (see Fiske, *Theatre Music*, 388-89), and if we are to believe a letter Chatterton wrote to his sister on 1 July 1770—quoted in John Nevil, *Thomas Chatterton* (London: Frederick Muller, 1948), 200-01—a score (lost) was at least partially completed, but the composer is not mentioned. There is no record of its actual performance.

A5 **APOLLO TURNED STROLLER**

Arnold has been credited with this composition; see the *Monthly Mirror* 10 (March 1803): 228. It was possibly written for Marylebone Gardens but there is no record of its actual performance. No libretto or music survives.

A6 **THE PORTRAIT**
Burletta in 3 parts
Libretto by George Colman, the elder (after Louis Anseaume, *Le Tableau parlant*, 1769)
First performed at Covent Garden, 22 November 1770
Printed keyboard-vocal score (London: Joseph Welcker, 28 November 1770; RISM A2325)
Singing characters: Isabella (Anne Catley), Columbine (Jane Thompson); Pantaloon (Edward Shuter), Leander (Frederick Reinhold).

A6.1 Overture

II. Rondo: Vivace 2/4, D

A6.2 Opening song (part 1): Isabella

A6.3 Opening song (part 2): Leander

A6.4 Opening song (part 3): Pantaloon

Text Incipits:
Part 1
    [Air: Isabella]   I'm pretty, I'm pretty
    [Air: Columbine]   Ah madam, reflect
    [Aria: Isabella]   Is that a form or feature
    [Air: Pantaloon]   How will I play the lover's part
    [Trio: Pantaloon,   Oh how painful 'tis to part
        Isabella, Columbine]

Part 2
    [Aria: Leander]   Tho' doom'd to tempt the fickle sea
    [Air: Columbine]   When beaus and smarts
    [Duet: Isabella, Leander] Leander was my daily theme
    [Air: Columbine]   Of all the evils

Part 3
    [Air: Pantaloon]   Tho' not in the bloom of my youth
    [Air: Leander]   Hang care and drive sorrow away
    [Trio: Isabella,   Away with all strife!
        Columbine, Leander]
    [Air: Isabella]   When lovers are old
    [Qt: Isabella, Columbine, Low at your feet, we thus entreat
        Leander, Pantaloon]

Arnold's animated solos wittily exploit the contrasts that come from words; Isabella's "I'm pretty" is an early example of an Arnold song where new thoughts receive new musical motives, and "Is that a form or feature" is indignant music of the kind we associate with Mozart's heroines. The trio ending part 1, where all three characters weep crocodile tears, sustains deception of feeling, and the "action ensemble" ending the opera, convincingly expresses a sense of acceleration and gathering energy, nearly out of control. If Arnold's setting is different from Grétry's of the previous year, then both are modeled to some extent on the tripping, syllabic style of Pergolesi. Colman's retold plot concerns a young couple who unknowingly outwit the girl's lecherous, Argus-like guardian. A copy of the printed libretto (London: T. Becket and Co., 1770) is in the British Library: 1346.f.20; Larpent Ms. 313. The printed score lacks recitatives.

A7 **THE MAGNET**
Musical entertainment in 1 act; music not extant
Libretto by Dorothea Dubois
First performed at Marylebone Gardens, 27 June 1771

Arnold's music for this work was "entirely new" (*Public Advertiser*, 6 July 1771); the singers were Charles Bannister, Miss Thomas, and Jane Thompson. The magnet of the title is Honoria's virtue, which draws from Claudius a proposal of marriage. A copy of the printed libretto (London: T. Becket, 1771) is in the British Library: 1178.c.22; libretto reveals recitatives, 14 vocal numbers, lost; also overture.

A8 **THE CURE FOR DOTAGE**
Musical entertainment in 1 act; music not extant
Librettist unknown
First performed at Marylebone Gardens, 3 August 1771

According to the *Public Advertiser* of 3 August 1771, the singers were Charles Bannister, Frederick Reinhold, Miss Thomas, and Jane Thompson. The *Monthly Mirror* 10 (March 1803): 228 credits Arnold with this composition.

A9 **DON QUIXOTE**
Entertainment for music in 1 act; music not extant
Libretto by D. J. Piguenit (after Miguel de Cervantes's novel)
First performed at Marylebone Gardens, 30 June 1774

According to the *Morning Chronicle* of 1 July 1774, Arnold's music was "sprightly and agreeable"; Charles Dubellamy sang Don Quixote and Frederick Reinhold, Sancho. Piguenit's text is chiefly based on the episode where Don Quixote stands vigil over his arms in the inn yard (part 1, chapters 16 and 17). A copy of the printed libretto (London: C. D. Piguenit, 1774) is in the Bodleian Library: Vet.A5e.179; libretto reveals recitatives, "Symphony of Soft Music," 13 vocal numbers, lost; also overture.

A10 **THE WEATHERCOCK**
Pasticcio "musical entertainment" in 2 acts; music not extant
Libretto by Theodosius Forrest
First performed at Covent Garden, 17 October 1775

The *Morning Post* of 8 October 1775 judged the drama was "wretched" and the music "trite." The title refers to the theme of shifting fortunes in love. Forrest's preface states that the text was "only meant as a Vehicle for introducing several Airs." Arnold's overture created some interest, but the work only lasted three nights. A copy of the printed libretto (London: T. Evans, 1775) is in the Bodleian Library: Vet.A5e.1955(6); Larpent Ms. 392; printed libretto reveals recitatives, 19 vocal numbers, lost; also overture.

A11 APRIL DAY
Burletta in 3 acts; music not extant
Libretto by Kane O'Hara (after George Saville Carey's *The Magic Girdle*)
First performed at the Haymarket Little Theatre, 22 August 1777

The text of *April Day* is based on the popular eighteenth-century theme of feigned magic. According to the libretto, Arnold's score included an "Incantation Recitative, accompanied by Magical Musick." This work received only two performances: newspaper critics found the comedy dull but the music was liked (*Morning Chronicle*, August 23: "The music is richly dramatic"; *Morning Post*, August 23: "The airs are in general novel, and truly harmonious; the recitative as characteristic, and forcibly set as the language would possibly admit of"). A copy of the printed libretto (London: G. Kearsley, 1777) is in the British Library: 643.e.6(11); libretto reveals recitatives, "Dialogue in Music," 22 vocal numbers, lost; also overture.

A12 THE ENRAGED MUSICIAN (UT PICTURA POESIS!)
Musical entertainment in 1 act
George Colman, the elder (after William Hogarth's engraving)
First performed at the Haymarket Little Theatre, 18 May 1789
Printed keyboard-vocal score (London: Longman and Broderip, 20 June 1789, as op. 31; RISM A2243)
Singing characters: Castruccina (Elizabeth Bannister), Piccolina (Mrs. Plomer), Milkmaid (Georgina George); Castruccio (A. Chambers), Quaver (Maria Iliff), Knife-grinder (William Reeve); street-criers (James Mathews, William [?] Chapman, John Johnson).

A12.1   Overture

II-III. Moderato 3/4-6/8, D

A12.2   Opening recitative (scene 1): Castruccio

A12.3. Opening recitative (scene 2): Quaver

Text Incipits:
Scene 1

[Recit: Castruccio]	Ah? Basta! Bene Castruccina
[Air: Castruccio]	Non termer [Ferdinando Bertoni, from *Demofoonte*, 1765]
[Recit: Castruccio]	Come now begin
[Aria: Piccolina]	Flutt'ring, flutt'ring spread thy purple pinions
[Recit: Castruccio]	Silence Welch goats?
[Air: Castruccina]	Alas and woe to Fanny
[Recit: Castruccio]	Divino! 'tis the music of the spheres
[Trio: Castruccio Castruccina, Piccolina]	Oh vat a happy day

Scene 2

[Recit: Quaver]	Here lives sweet Castruccina!
[Air: Quaver]	In air, serenata
[Recit: Quaver, Milkmaid]	But who shall be the bearer of this letter?
[Air: Milkmaid]	Ye nymphs and sylvan Gods
[Recit: Quaver]	This note tells Castruccina
[Air: Knife-grinder]	Knives to grind!
[Recit: Knife-grinder, Quaver]	Ha! Are you there?
[Recit: Quaver]	A pleasant trick
[Air: Quaver]	O thou whose charms [Charles Dibdin (new)]
[Recit: Quaver, Castruccina]	But see, the window opens
[Duet: Castruccina, Quaver]	Painful to part
[Recit: Castruccio]	Confound your noises!
[Sxt: Castruccio, Quaver, Milkmaid, street-criers]	O curse your din you've shut me in

Arnold developed the art of burlesque, both by the novelties he introduced into his score, such as the street-criers' sextet, and by imitative effects such as the sounds of artillery, all of which wittily underline the text. Equally, the music parodies the conventions of *opera seria* and ballad opera. A copy of the printed libretto (London: T. Cadell, 1789) is in the British Library: 11777.c.23; Larpent Ms. 826.

B / Mainpiece Operas with Spoken Dialogue

B1   **THE MAID OF THE MILL**
Pasticcio "comic opera" in 3 acts
Libretto by Isaac Bickerstaffe (after Samuel Richardson, *Pamela*, 1740, and John Fletcher and William Rowley, *The Maid in the Mill*, 1623)
First performed at Covent Garden, 31 January 1765
Printed keyboard-vocal score (London: R. Bremner, 31 January 1765; RISM A2286)
"Piano-Forte Magazine" edition (London: Harrison, Cluse & Co., as nos. 80-83, ca. 1799; RISM A2288)
Printed flute score (London: R. Bremner, 1765; copy in University of London Music Library: M788.5)

Numbers by Arnold:

B1.1 Quartetto (act 1): Patty, Giles, Ralph, Fanny

B1.2 Song (act 2): Giles

B1.3* + Song (act 2): Theodosia

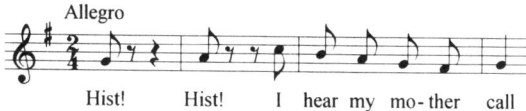

B1.4 Quintetto ending act 1: Sir Henry Sycamore, Giles, Patty, Theodosia, Lord Aimworth

Other numbers drawn from Girolamo Aboo, Johann Christian Bach, Legrenzio Ciampi, Gioacchino Cocchi, Egidio Duni, Baldassare Galuppi, Felice de Giardini, Johann Hasse, Nicolò Jommelli, Thomas Alexander Erskine, 6th Earl of Kelly, Elector of Saxony, Gaetano Latilla, Vicenzo Martini, Pierre Monsigny, Giovanni Pergolesi, François Philador, Niccolò Piccini, Rinaldo da Capua, Domenico Scarlatti, Leonardo Vinci. For details of the borrowings, see Fiske, *Theatre Music*, 607-08. Note also P. T. Dirck "Musical Drama and Artistic Whole: The Necessity for Special Criteria" (an essay centered on Isaac Bickerstaffe), *Studies in Burke and His Time* 15 (1974): 277-86.

Arnold's first opera, this work reveals his ability to create a successful full-scale dramatic work and is a sampler of "action finales" in English opera. The borrowings are chiefly from Italian arias in the new *galant* idiom and from relatively unknown French operas. Its popularity was maintained throughout the eighteenth century; Bickerstaffe's plot took note of the recent fashion for exploring marital and master-servant relations. Busby, *Anecdotes*, 1:90-91, claimed that Arnold arranged the score "for the inconsiderable sum of *twelve* pounds."

For unchanged reissues of Bremner's vocal score, see RISM A2287, 89. The starred/crossed item was published separately (RISM A2290) and there is a manuscript copy in Glasgow University Library: B:22z.29, pp. 182-83.

A Thematic Index

A copy of the printed libretto (London: J. Newberry and others, 1765) is in the Bodleian Library: Douce PP 125(1); it was widely reprinted in contemporary and early nineteenth-century collections.

B2 **THE SPANISH BARBER (THE FRUITLESS PRECAUTION)**
Comic opera in 3 acts
Libretto by George Colman, the elder (after Pierre-Augustin Beaumarchais, *Le Barbier de Seville*, 1775)
First performed at the Haymarket Little Theatre, 30 August 1777
Printed keyboard-vocal score (London: John Bland, 24 July 1782, as op. 17; RISM A2352)
"Piano-Forte Magazine" edition (London: Harrison, Cluse & Co., as vol. 18, no. 5, ca. 1799; RISM A2353)
Printed flute score (London: Harrison & Co., 1 October 1784; RISM A2354)
Singing characters: Rosina (Elizabeth Harper), Lazarillo (John Edwin), Dr. Bartholo (William Parsons), Tall-Boy (John Palmer), Argus (Ralph Wewitzer), Basil (? Massey)

B2.1 Overture "El Fandango"

B2.2 Opening song (act 1): Lazarillo

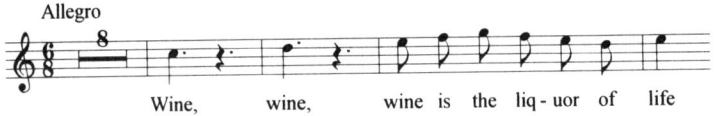

B2.3 Opening aria (act 2): Basil

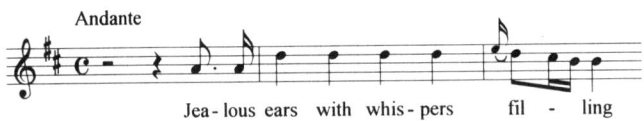

B2.4 Opening song (act 3): Rosina

Text incipits:
Act 1
  [Air: Lazarillo]   Wine, wine is the liquor of life
  [Air: Rosina]   Dungeons and fetters may restrain
  [Air: Lazarillo]   An humble batchelor is nigh
  [Air: Lazarillo]   Your toupee I can twirl
  [Air: Rosina]   Tell-tale eyes ["Je suis Lindor"]
  [Trio: Dr. Bartholo,   Zounds, rascal speak out
    Tall-Boy, Argus]

Act 2
  [Aria: Basil]   Jealous ears with whispers filling
  [Air: Rosina]   * When with tenderness we languish ["Medea and Jason" (apparently from George Colman's ballet of 1781, music by "Gluck")]
  [Air: Rosina]   * Love, the soul firing
  [Air: Dr. Bartholo]   Can Leon or fair Arragon

Act 3
  [Air: Rosina]   * Ah, how hapless is the maid
  [Fnle: Lazarillo, Basil   Sickly dotage to restrain
    Rosina, Bartholo]

This opera sustained public interest for twenty years (partly because Beaumarchais's play with its evident class-conscious sympathy was a great success in England) but, surprisingly, Arnold's score seems to have waited five years for publication. If the mixture of comic and serious styles is typical of English opera, then in the background lay the heritage of Italian opera. Lazarillo's (Figaro) barber song ("Your toupee"), for example, relies on the rapid, syllabic *buffo* style reminiscent of Pergolesi, while Rosina's solos are mainly associated with the formal opening ritornellos, melodic grace, and melismatic singing of Italianate, "amoroso" or lyric arias. The ensemble concluding act 1 contains amusing onamatopoeic interjections (sneezing and yawning). The "Fandango" overture established the Spanish setting and apparently a "storm" *entr'acte* connected acts 1 and 2 (*Morning Chronicle*, 1 September 1777). See my "Samuel Arnold's *The Spanish Barber*," *Early Music New Zealand* 4 (1985): 11-14.

Starred items were published separately (Hoskins, *Arnold*, 2:65-66; RISM A2355-58). An edition of the song-words (London: T. Cadell, 1779) is in the British Library: 1609/5880(11); Larpent Ms. 436 (transcribed in Burnim, *Colman 1*, 4).

B3   **SUMMER AMUSEMENT (AN ADVENTURE AT MARGATE)**
Pasticcio "comic opera" in 3 acts
Libretto by Miles Peter Andrews and William Augustus Miles
First performed at the Haymarket Little Theatre, 1 July 1779
Printed keyboard-vocal score (London: S. A. & P. Thompson, 1779; RISM A2359)
Singing characters: Amelia (Elizabeth Harper), Lady Juniper (Lydia Webb), Captain Surat (Charles Bannister), Etiquette (John Edwin), Spruce (Philip Lamash), Sir James Juniper (William Parsons), Melville (Charles Wood); chorus of fishermen

A Thematic Index

B3.1 * Overture Allegro

II. Rondo [tempo unmarked] 6/8, G

B3.2   Opening chorus (act 1): fishermen

B3.3   Opening song (act 2): Amelia

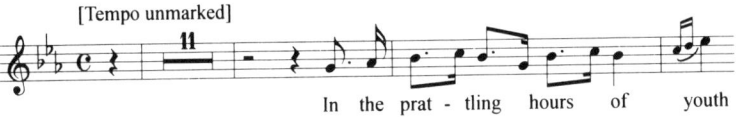

B3.4   Opening song (act 3): Captain Surat

Text incipits:

Act 1

[Chos & solo: fishermen, Capt. Surat]	* Haul, haul away [& solo "Happy Island"*; unison chorus]
[Air: Capt. Surat]	* The wand'ring sailor
[Air: Etiquette]	* Without a man to take the lead
[Air: Spruce]	When madam ["French air"]
[Air: Amelia]	To ease my heart [Thomas Arne, "Scotch Gavotte" (in the overture to *Thomas and Sally*, 1760)]
[Duet: Lady Juniper, Sir James]	* If husbands wish for happy lives
[Fnle: Surat, Amelia, Lady Juniper, Sir James]	Hark the sprightly sounds begin

Act 2

[Air: Amelia]	* In the prattling hours of youth
[Air: Etiquette]	* Neatest of pretty feet [Thomas Arne, "Take me Jenny," *Musical Magazine* 2 (1768)]
[Air: Melville]	Thou hast play'd ["Had awa frae me, Donald"]
[Air: Capt. Surat]	Go high, go low [Charles Dibdin, "Blow high, blow low," *The Seraglio* (1776)]
[Aria: Amelia]	* How hard our hapless lot
[Fnle: Surat, Amelia, Lady Juniper, Etiquette]	Come ye venal slaves of war

Act 3
    [Air: Capt. Surat]   * If I'm the happy man
    [Air: Melville]   What means that downcast look [Thomas Arne, "Excuse for a love slip," *Vocal Melody* 2 (ca. 1746)]
    [Air: Lady Juniper]   * When a lady of ton
    [Aria: Amelia]   Let not love [Tommaso Giordani, "Let not age," *a favorite Cantata, Sung by Mrs. Weichsell at Vauxhall*, 1773]
    [Fnle: Etiquette, Surat, Amelia, Melville]   * Ladies and gentlemen, this is a set

Amelia's "How hard our hapless lot" is vocally the most expressive number, with yearning phrases and coloratura (the opening ritornello is scored for solo oboe and bassoon). There is a resemblance between the opening of the act 1 finale and the last movement of Arnold's Sonata op. 13, book 1, no. 7. In the second movement of the overture solos for two oboes occur in alternation with tutti passages.

The starred items were published separately (Hoskins, *Arnold*, 2:75-78; RISM 2360-71). A copy of the printed song-words (London: T. Cadell, 1779) is in the Music Library, Yale University. The libretto was not published, but a synopsis of the plot appears in the *London Chronicle*, 1-3 July 1779; Larpent Ms. 485. Facsimile of vocal score (New York: Belwin Mills, 1978).

B4   **BARON KINKVERVANKOTSDORSPRAKINGATCHDERN**
Pasticcio "musical comedy" in 3 acts; music not extant
Libretto by Miles Peter Andrews (after Elizabeth Craven, *A Tale for Christmas*, 1779)
First performed at the Haymarket Little Theatre, 9 July 1781

According to the *Morning Herald* of 10 July 1781: "Much was expected from the Music, which is a compilation of *high and low* Dutch tunes, but we are sorry to say that it failed throughout in effect. Two songs only engaged the attention of the audience." The newspaper reviewers were equally severe on the text and production. The third (and final) performance was stopped mid-way when the audience rioted. Arnold's choice of Dutch music is not known; the story is set in Holland. Copies of the libretto and song-words (both London: T. Cadell, 1781) are in the Bodleian Library: Malone B.3(5); Douce S.134 (3); they reveal 14 vocal numbers, lost; also overture.

B5   **THE CASTLE OF ANDALUSIA**
Pasticcio "comic opera" in 3 acts; an alteration of *The Banditti*, 28 November 1781
Libretto by John O'Keeffe, perhaps inspired by the "banditti" paintings of Salvator Rosa
First performed at Covent Garden, 2 November 1782
Printed keyboard-vocal score (London: John Bland, 19 November 1782, as op. 20; RISM A2220)
Reissue of Bland's score (London: G. Goulding, ca. 1796; RISM A2221)
"Piano-Forte Magazine" edition (London: Harrison, Cluse & Co., as vol. 7, nos. 108-12, ca. 1799; RISM A2222)

Printed flute score (London: John Bland, 19 November 1782; RISM A2224)
Printed guitar score (Dublin: J. Lee, ca. 1785; RISM A2223)

Numbers by Arnold:

B5.1 Overture

  II. Andante con espressione 3/4, D
  III. Allegro 6/8, D

B5.2 + Opening ATB chorus of banditti (act 1)

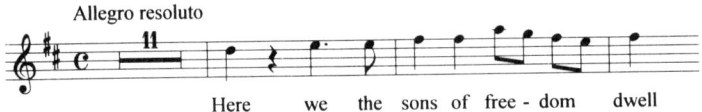

B5.3* + Song (act 1): Ramirez

B5.4* Song (act 1): Alphonso

B5.5* Song (act 1): Pedrillo

B5.6 Aria (act 1): Victoria [flute and strings]

B5.7 Quintetto ending act 1: Don Scipio, Isabel, Pedrillo, Fernando, Lorenza

B5.8 Air (act 2): Fernando

B5.9 * Duet (act 2): Victoria, Fernando

B5.10 * Air (act 3): Pedrillo

B5.11 Aria (act 3): Victoria [flute and strings]

B5.12 Glee (act 3): Victoria, Fernando, Alphonso

B5.13 Glee ending act 3: Victoria, Lorenza, Fernando, Pedrillo, Don Scipio

Other numbers were drawn from Thomas Arne, Ferdinando Bertoni, Carolan, Felice de Giardini, Tommaso Giordani, George Frideric Handel, Mattia Vento; for details on the borrowings, see Fiske, *Theatre Music*, 600-01. **B5.9** is a version of "Ah what tender soft emotions" from Arnold's oratorio *Abimelech* (1768), where it is sung as a reconciliation duet by Abraham and Sarah.

Arnold's last pasticcio *The Banditti*, written for Thomas Harris, the Covent Garden manager in 1781, failed, but Covent Garden revised it the next year as *The Castle of Andalusia*, in which form it rivaled *The Duenna* in popularity and stayed in the repertory for a good half-century, though with no benefit to the composer (see Landon, *Haydn*, 3:281). O'Keeffe's pseudo-Gothic drama was a novelty in its day, and Arnold's music is remarkable for the "action ensemble" ending act 1, and for two soprano arias that express the inner aspects of the text. In his choice of borrowings, Arnold's invariable method is to employ an element of parody. For a full discussion of this work, including a table of vocal music, see my critical introduction to the facsimile reproduction of Bland's score, *Music for London Entertainment* (series C, vol. 5, 1991), ix-xvi.

Starred items were published separately (Hoskins, *Arnold*, 2:110-15; RISM A2226-27, also AA2225a-271). Manuscript copies of B5.2-3 (crossed) are in the Royal College of Music: 2108 (SH 1948), ff. 48, 52; there is a copy of B5.9 in the Ewing Library Glasgow: Ms.R.d.48, f. 6v.

The music of *The Banditti* is not extant, but a copy of the printed song-words (London: T. Cadell, 1782) is in the British Library: 11777.c.6. The text survives in Larpent Ms. 577 (for a synopsis of the plot, see the *Public Advertiser*, 29 November 1781). Copies of the printed song-words (London: T. Cadell, 1782) and libretto (London: T. N. Longman, 1794) of *The Castle of Andalusia* are in the Bodleian Library: Douce S.134(15); Vet.A5e.1446(4); Larpent Ms. 605 is reproduced in *Music for London Entertainment* (series C, vol. 5). *The London Stage* lists *The Castle of Andalusia* as fifteenth in popularity among mainpieces produced 1776-1800.

B6   **TWO TO ONE**
Comic opera in 3 acts
Libretto by George Colman, the younger
First performed at the Haymarket Little Theatre, 19 June 1784
Printed keyboard-vocal score (London: Harrison & Co., 5 July 1784, nos. 30-33 of "New Musical Magazine" as op. 24; RISM A2396)
Printed flute score (London: Harrison & Co., 14 August 1784; RISM A2397)
Singing characters: Charlotte (Elizabeth Bannister), Tippet (Georgina George); Crape (William Davies), Capt. Dupely (Charles Bannister), Dicky Ditto (John Edwin), Dupely (Richard Wilson)

B6.1   Overture

II. Andante 3/4, D
III. Allegro 9/8, D

B6.2 Opening song (act 1): Charlotte

B6.3 Opening song (act 2): Captain Dupely

B6.4 Opening song (act 3): Tippet

Text incipits:
Act 1
    [Air: Charlotte]   Pensive I mourn my absent swain [oboe and strings]
    [Air: Tippet]   If a coxcomb all starch [strings]
    [Aria: Charlotte]   Welcome, sweet fancy
    [Air: Tippet]   * How happy the woman
    [Air: Crape]   * There is a chambermaid ["Peggy of Derby O"]
    [Air: Tippet]   Hang your humdrum loobies!
    [Duet: Tippet, Crape]   Come, little Tippet ["Herring and salt"]

Act 2
    [Air: Capt. Dupely]   Talk not of your dirty acres
    [Air: Capt. Dupely]   The study intense
    [Air: Dicky Ditto]   A mercer I am ["Little Bingo" (ca. 1780)]
    [Air: Dicky Ditto]   Adzooks old crusty ["Yankee Doodle" (ca. 1767)]
    [Aria: Charlotte]   Uncertainty with chequer'd crew [oboes, strings]
    [Air: Tippet]   * John tripp'd up the stairs ["Duncan Gray"]

    [Aria: Charlotte]   Smile, kindest fortune
    [Air: Dupely]   Once on a time ["As Roger came tapping at Dolly's window"]
    [Trio: Dupely, Charlotte   Then come indoors to make love
      Tippet]

Act 3
    [Air: Tippet]   London ladies walk the streets ["Maggie Lauder"]
    [Air: Tippet]   At an inn so merry ["Venetian ballad"; strings]
    [Air: Charlotte]   When cruel parents [Philip Hayes, "The Highland laddie" (ca. 1780)]
    [Air: Capt. Dupely]   How clumsy the airs of a cit
    [Air: Dupely]   When a lover's in the wind ["The auld wife ayont the fire"]
    [Fnle: Dupely, Capt. Dupely, Bobbing about to the fiddle ["Ay, let us a'to the bridal"]
      Charlotte, Tippet]

This work is remarkable for its use of folksong, including "Yankee Doodle," which is here printed for the first time. Arnold's own music is concentrated on the solos given to the two female characters. Charlotte's love-lorn arias contain expressive coluratura and Tippet's first solo is a satire on the minuet and country dance. The second movement of the overture begins with solo horns "sustonuto"; episodes for solo oboe and bassoon follow.

Starred items were published separately (Hoskins, *Arnold*, 2:130-31; RISM A2398-99). Copies of the printed song-words (London: T. Cadell, 1784) and unauthorized libretto (Dublin: W. Wilson, 1785) are in the Bodleian Library: Douce S.134(9), M. Adds. 108f.99(4); Larpent Ms. 631.

B7   **TURK AND NO TURK**
Comic opera in 3 acts
Libretto by George Colman, the younger
First performed at the Haymarket Little Theatre, 9 July 1785
Printed vocal-keyboard score (London: T. Skillern, 12 August 1785, as op. 28; RISM A2395)
Singing characters: Fib (Georgina George), Lady Simple (Lydia Webb), Emily (Elizabeth Bannister); Presto (John Edwin), Sir Roger Ramble (Charles Bannister), Moneo (John Bannister)

B7.1   Overture

     II. Un poco andante 3/4, D
     III. Rondo: Allegro 2/4, D

B7.2   Opening song (act 1): Fib

B7.3   Opening song (act 2): Lady Simple

B7.4   Opening song (act 3): Sir Roger Ramble

Text incipits:

Act 1
- [Air: Fib] — You may slight me who's afraid
- [Aria: Fib] — Only look at me maids [oboe and strings]
- [Air: Presto] — I'm worse than poor debtors ["The tailor done over" (ca. 1785)]
- [Duet: Presto, Fib] — List, little Fibby ["Hunting the hare"]

Act 2
- [Air: Lady Simple] — Some talk of Cherokees Sir ["The British grenadiers"]
- [Air: Presto] — My master a gay pulpiteer ["There was an old woman"]
- [Air: Emily] — Why did Damon's eyes so bright [strings]
- [Air: Emily] — Ah parents, ere your glass is run ["Life penitente"]
- [Air: Fib] — Jonothan a-wooing went
- [Qt: Lady Simple, Presto, Emily, Fib] — Your master, young man, may a lass adore

Act 3
- [Air: Sir Roger] — You my spruce little Mathew [horns and strings]
- [Duet: Sir Roger, Moneo] — As through the clouds rolls rumbling thunder
- [Air: Presto] — Look maids! I cock my hat
- [Air: Fib] — Once in a chimney corner snug
- [Air: Emily] — When e'er the evening dew descends [Maurice Greene, "Sweet Annie frae the sea beach came," *The Chaplet: Being a collection of twelve English songs* (1738)]
- [Fnle: Sir Roger, Emily, Presto, Fib] — Jocund fill the flowing bowl ["La sposa Persiana - Turkish dance"]

Additional songs
- [Aria: Fib] — When e'er a lover sighs
- [Air: Emily] — Ah parents, e'er your glass is run [new version by Arnold]

The plot revolves around young Ramble, who disguises himself as a Turk in order to deceive Emma's antiquarian father. According to Colman, *Random Records*, 2:267, the text was destroyed, but a manuscript copy survives in Larpent Ms. 704 (transcribed in Tasch, *Colman 2*, 1). Most remarkable is the unusually high soprano part in solos composed by Arnold for Georgina George. Presto's "Look maids! I cock my hat," with its initial two-measure phrases alternating A major and E major, is an excellent example of Arnold's simulated folk-style. Arnold's version of "The British grenadiers" probably came from the single sheet folio of 1770. The overture constitutes one of Arnold's most sophisticated orchestral works; the opening theme recurs as a second subject of the finale. A copy of the printed song-words (London: T. Cadell, 1785) is in the Bodleian Library: Douce S.134.

B8   THE SIEGE OF CURZOLA
Comic opera in 3 acts
Libretto by John O'Keeffe (after Richard Knolles's *General History of the Turk*, 1603)
First performed at the Haymarket Little Theatre, 12 August 1786
Printed keyboard-vocal score (London: Longman & Broderip, 5 September 1786, as op. 29; RISM A2338)

Singing characters: Baba (Giovanna Sestini), Teresa (Georgina George), Stella (Elizabeth Bannister), Antonietta (Lydia Webb); Podesto (Cockran Booth), Cricolo (John Edwin), Jollyboat (William Brett), Weatherbang (William Meadows), Junk (William Davies)

B8.1   Overture

   II. Andante 3/4, D
   III. March 2/2, D

B8.2   "Dances immediately after the overture"

   II. Vivace 6/8, D
   III. Moderato 2/4, G [flute and "pizzicato" strings]

B8.3   Opening song (act 1): Podesto

B8.4   Opening song (act 2): Baba

B8.5   Opening song (act 3): Teresa

Text incipits:
Act 1
 [Air: Podesto]   Come follow, my lords and ladies gay ["The farmer of Taunton green"]
 [Aria: Baba]   Sweet ladies, look, admire, behold
 [Air: Teresa]   Oh when I was a little fool
 [Air: Cricolo]   My daddy was a good fellow
 [Air: Stella]   In fancy let nature delight [Thomas Arne (new)]

| [Sxt: Jollyboat Junk, Weatherbang, Podesto, Cricolo, Teresa] | There lives a maid at Wapping Wall |

Act 2
[Air: Baba]	See Flora's bowers
[Trio: Baba, Cricolo, Podesto]	Ah polite, debonaire
[Aria: Jollyboat]	The night comes on without a star
[Air: Teresa]	Though my dress perhaps is homely [oboe and strings]
[Fnle: Jollyboat, Junk, Cricolo, Teresa, Baba, Podesto, Weatherbang]	A coward mean as ever ran

Act 3
[Air: Teresa]	* Your wise men all declare
[Aria: Baba]	What sweet sensation [Luigi Cherubini, possibly from the lost opera buffa *La finta principessa* (1785)]
[Air: Weatherbang]	In May fifteen hundred eighty and eight
[Air: Cricolo]	The beacon flames, the Turks are come
[Air: Stella]	Go wild and fickle rover [solo violin and "cembalo"]
[Qt: Weatherbang, Antonietta, Junk, Jollyboat]	Sweet girls, don't depend on your conquering charms
[Fnle: Weatherbang, Junk, Baba, Cricolo, Teresa, Antonietta, Stella, Jollyboat]	Let's all sit down to supper boys

This work contains animated solos and a witty trio in act 2 which is a satire on the minuet as a dance. The rhythmic characteristics of the second movement of the overture can be matched with the central movement of Arnold's *Six Overtures* op. 8, no. 2; both make use of colorful orchestral alternations. The starred song in act 3 is sung by Florina in *The Birth Day* (C13); this item was published separately (Hoskins, *Arnold*, 2:149-50; RISM A2339-41). RISM A2339 is published in full score for oboes, horns, and strings.

There is a synopsis of O'Keeffe's pseudo-historic plot in the *Public Advertiser* and *Morning Chronicle* of 14 August 1786. An edition of the printed song-words (London: T. Cadell, 1785) is in the Music Library, Yale University; Larpent Ms. 743.

B9   INKLE AND YARICO
Comic opera in 3 acts
Libretto by George Colman, the younger (after Richard Steele's *The Spectator*, Tuesday 13 March 1711, via Richard Ligon's *History of the Island of Barbados*, 1673; also ? Weddell's *Incle and Yarico: A Tragedy of Three Acts*, 1742)
First performed at the Haymarket Little Theatre, 4 August 1787
Printed keyboard-vocal score (London: Longman & Broderip, 6 September 1787, as op. 30; RISM A2261)
Printed flute score (London: Longman & Broderip, 3 December 1788; RISM A2262)
Printed guitar score (London: Longman & Broderip, 6 January 1789; RISM A2263)

Singing characters: Yarico (Elizabeth Kemble), Wowski (Georgina George), Narcissa (Elizabeth Bannister), Patty (Ann Forster); Mate (William Meadows), Trudge (John Edwin), Inkle (John Bannister), Campley (William Davies); chorus of sailors

B9.1 * Overture

    II. Andante 3/4, G
    III. Sprightly 2/4, D ["Have you seen the muffin man?"]

B9.2   Opening song (act 1): Mate

B9.3   Opening song (act 2): Narcissa

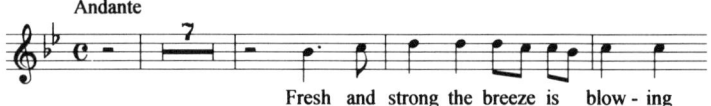

B9.4   Opening song (act 3): Patty

Text incipits:

Act 1

[Air: Chos: Mate, sailors]	+ The Achilles, tho' christen'd [unison chorus]
[Air: Trudge]	* + A voyage o'er seas ["Last Valentine's day"]
[Aria: Yarico]	* When the chace of day is done
[Duet: Inkle, Yarico]	* Oh say, simple maid ["Oh say, bonny lass" (ca. 1780)]
[Air: Wowski]	* + White man never go away ["One day I heard Mary say" (ca. 1740)]
[Duet: Wowski, Trudge]	Wampum sampum

Act 2

[Air: Narcissa]	* + Fresh and strong the breeze is blowing
[Air: Patty]	This maxim let ev'ryone hear
[Aria: Narcissa]	* Mars wou'd oft his conquests ["Since 'tis vain to think of flying," possibly by Giovanni Paisiello]
[Aria: Campley]	Why shou'd I vain fears discover
[Air: Wowski]	* + Remember when we walk'd alone

[Air: Yarico]	* Our grotto was the sweetest place
[Trio: Campley, Narcissa, Patty]	Your colinets and arietts

Act 3
[Air: Patty]	Tho' lovers, like marksmen, all aim at the heart
[Air: Trudge]	* + A clerk I was in London gay
[Fnle: Campley, Narcissa, Trudge, Yarico, Patty]	* Come, let us dance and sing ["La belle Catharine"]

Additional songs composed for J. Johnstone (Inkle) at Covent Garden, 22 October 1788

B9.5

Printed full score for horns, clarinets and strings (London: Longman & Broderip, 29 December 1788; RISM A2277)

B9.6

Printed full score for horns, oboes and strings (London: Longman & Broderip, 29 December 1788; RISM A2278)

This opera, popular for at least fifty years, may be regarded in its subject matter as a direct reflection of the anti-slavery spirit that surged through England in the last years of the eighteenth century. Inkle, an English adventurer, does not know whether to marry a rich heiress or his Jamaican mistress, Yarico, who has saved his life. He yields to Yarico, though avarice gives him a sharp tussle. Arnold's music explores little of the moral character of the opera, except perhaps in Yarico's "Our grotto was the sweetest place" when she remembers her past joy; the extreme simplicity of the harmony, the murmuring orchestral responses to the vocal line, and doubling of the vocal part by the violins at the unison contribute to the artless sincerity of her expression. The second movement of the overture opens with a solo for "octave flute" (piccolo) and bassoon, and the rondo finale makes use of wind instruments in the episodes; the vaudeville finale ending act 3 is based on the rondo theme.

The additional songs for Johnstone were presumably intended to replace Yarico's two solos, which were not sung. Charlotte Chapman was not a musician and, according to the *Morning Post* of 23 October 1788, she performed only "Oh say, simple maid." We learn from the *Morning Chronicle* of 23 October 1788 that Johnstone sang the new songs "with great taste and effect."

Starred items were published separately (Hoskins, *Arnold*, 2:154-59; RISM A2264-81, also AA2264a-78a). Crossed items (+) are manuscript copies found in the British Library: Add. Ms. 25076, ff. 3-6; Add. Ms. 25078, f. 19v; Add. Ms. 34126, f. 79v. A copy of the printed libretto (London: G. G. J. and J. Robinson, 1787) is in the Bodleian Library: Vet.A5e.1150; Larpent Ms. 782. The libretto was widely reprinted in contemporary and early nineteenth-century collections, and there is a modern facsimile of the vocal score (New York: Belwin

Mills, 1978). Lawrence M. Price, in his *Inkle and Yarico Album* (Berkeley: University of California Press, 1937), devotes several pages to Colman's version of the story; see also Barry Sutliffe's edition in *Plays by George Colman the Younger and Thomas Morton*, British and American Playwrights, 1750-1920 (Cambridge: Cambridge University Press, 1983).

B10   **THE BATTLE OF HEXHAM (DAYS OF OLD)**
Play in 3 acts
Libretto by George Colman, the younger (after Edward Hall, *Union of the Two Noble and Illustrate Families of York and Lancaster*, 1548, Holinshed's *Chronicles*, 1577, and William Shakespeare's *Henry VI* plays)
First performed at the Haymarket Little Theatre, 11 August 1789
Printed keyboard-vocal score (London: Longman & Broderip, 14 September 1789, as op. 32; RISM A2210)
Singing characters: Adeline (Charlotte Goodall); Gregory (John Edwin), Drummer (William Moss), Fool (Robert Palmer), Robber Captain (Charles Bannister); chorus of soldiers; robbers; villagers

B10.1 * Overture

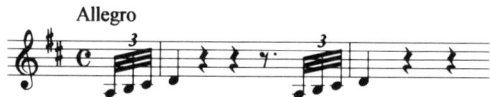

     II. Slow march 4/4, D
     III. Rondo: [tempo unmarked] 2/4, D

B10.2   Opening song (act 1): Adeline

B10.3 * "March for the House of York" (act 1)

B10.4   Opening glee [3 voices] (act 2): robbers

B10.5 Opening song (act 3): Fool

Text incipits:
Act 1
    [Air: Adeline]   The mincing step
    [Air: Gregory]   Ah, what's a valiant hero?
    [Solo & Chos: drummer, soldiers]   My tight fellow soldiers [ATB? chorus]
    [Chos: soldiers]   Strike, strike, strike [ATB]

Act 2
    [Glee: robbers]   * When Arthur first in court [John Callcott, "Chearful Glee," 3 voices (ca. 1789)]
    [Catch: robbers]   * Lurk o'er the greensward [Thomas Arne, "Buzz quoth the blue fly," 4 voices, *The Fairy Prince* (1771)]

Act 3
    [Air: Fool]   To arms, to arms, when captains cry
    [Roundelay: villagers]   Drifted snow no more is seen [unison chorus]
    [Aria: Robber Captain]   When the stout freebooters prowl
    [Air: Gregory]   * In an old quiet parish ["Four and twenty fiddlers all in a row"]
    [Fnle: soldiers, villagers]   England, to thyself be true [SATB]

This work is the first hybrid opera by Arnold, and it remained popular for over thirty years. Colman's language and setting emulates Shakespeare's historical dramas. The emphasis on the chorus is an experimental departure from the norm of the period. Trumpet solos occur in alternation with tutti passages throughout the overture. Trumpets and fife assume considerable importance in Gregory's first song and in the theatrical chorus of soldiers ending act 1. "When the stout freebooters prowl" is written in three staves to accommodate the dense string writing (including independent viola). Gregory's last song was John Edwin's specialty; this version had been published in 1788 as "Edwin's New Four and Twenty Fiddlers."

Starred items were published separately (Hoskins, *Arnold*, 2:167-69; RISM A2211-15, also AA2213a). A copy of the authorized printed libretto (London: Longman, Hurst, Rees, and Orme, 1808) is in the British Library: 643.h.14(15), and a copy of the song-words (London: T. Cadell, 1789) can be found in the Bodleian Library: Vet.A5e.3298; Larpent Ms. 840.

B11   **NEW SPAIN (LOVE IN MEXICO)**
Comic opera in 3 acts
Libretto by John Scawen
First performed at the Haymarket Little Theatre, 16 July 1790
Printed keyboard-vocal score (London: Longman & Broderip, 13 September 1790, as op. 33; RISM A2314)

Singing characters: Leonora (Charlotte Goodall), Flora (Louisa Fontenelle), Julia (Maria Iliff), Iscagli (Elizabeth Bannister), Ulah (Mrs. Edwards), Indian attendant (? Edwards); Don Garcias (William Waterhouse), Alkmonoak (Charles Bannister), Don Juan (William Davies), Don Lopez (Thomas Ryder), Secretary (Robert Palmer), Fabio (John Bannister); chorus of Indians

B11.1   Overture

II. Andante 3/4, D
III. Allegro 6/8, D

B11.2   Opening song (act 1): Leonora

B11.3   Opening song (act 2): Fabio

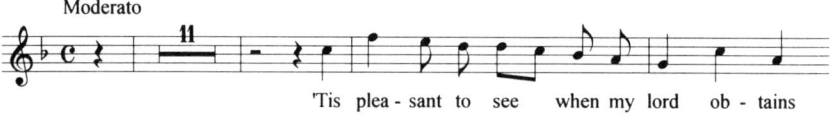

B11.4   Opening song (act 3): Iscagli

Text incipits:
Act 1
  [Air: Leonora]   With many a sad, intrusive doubt oppress'd
  [Aria: Don Garcias]   Now Cynthia rode in silver car
  [Air: Alkmonoak]   I have lost her
  [Trio: Don Juan, Don Garcias,   Three pilgrims at love's sacred shrine
    Alkmonoak]
  [Duet: Don Lopez, Secretary]   Off, you dog, or I'll crack your crown
  [Air: Flora]   As the soldier lad
  [Air: Fabio]   Two maidens my heart transfix'd
  [Qnt: Leonora, Julia, Juan,   The morning breeze which sweeps the grove
    Flora, Fabio]

Act 2
  [Air: Fabio]   'Tis pleasant to see when my lord obtains
  [Air: Alkmonoak]   Thou that liv'st in every port

B / MAINPIECE OPERAS WITH SPOKEN DIALOGUE

[Duet: Iscagli, Ulah] — To shun the gay and gaudy bow'r
[Aria: Iscagli] — There to muse and there to sigh
[Air: Julia] — When the blithe village maids
[Qnt: Leonora, Lopez, Garcias, Fabio, Julia] — How keen the glance

Act 3
[Aria: Iscagli] — Thou sandy bourne, upon whose faithless breast
[Air: Ulah] — * +What boots it where thy soldier lies
[Air & Chos: Alkmonoak; Indians] — Do thou, sweet sympathy, my voice convey [ATB chorus]
[Air: Alkmonoak] — The sun sets at night
[Chos: Indians] — In his ambush wisely dark [ATB]
[Fnle: Iscagli, Leonora, Julia, Garcia, Juan, Alkmonoak, Lopez, Flora] — Who in absence long have known

The plot pivots on Leonora who, disguised as a soldier, follows Don Garcias to Mexico. There she is promoted to lieutenant-governor and becomes embroiled in an Indian uprising. The piece ran only nine nights; Arnold's functional music created little interest.

The starred/crossed item was published separately (RISM AA2314a) and a manuscript copy can be found in the National Library of Wales: Egsair 13. The second movement of the overture and six vocal items have cues for woodwind entries; Iscagli's "There to muse" includes bassoons and contrabassoons.

A copy of the printed libretto (London: G. G. J. and J. Robinson, 1790) can be found in the British Library: 643.e.19(5); Larpent Ms. 874.

B12   THE SURRENDER OF CALAIS
Play in 3 acts
Libretto by George Colman, the younger (after Froissart's *Chronicles*)
First performed at the Haymarket Little Theatre, 30 July 1791
Printed keyboard-vocal score (London: Preston & Son, 1791, as op. 33; RISM A2372)
Printed flute score (London: Preston & Son, 1791; RISM A2373)
Printed flute score (selections) (London: Longman & Broderip, ca. 1795; RISM AA2373a)
Singing characters: Madelon (Maria Bland); O'Carrol (John Johnstone), La Gloire (John Bannister); chorus of soldiers; inhabitants of Calais

B12.1 * Overture

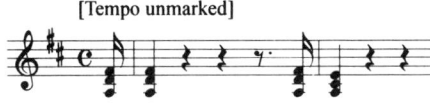

II. Quick march 2/2, D

B12.2 Opening chorus (act 1): Sergeant and soldiers

B12.3 Opening duet (act 2): Madelon

B12.4 March "When the Queen enters" (act 2)

B12.5 Opening song (act 3): O'Carrol

B12.6 March "When the citizens are led to execution" (act 3)

Text incipits:
Act 1
    [Air & Chos: Sergeant, soldiers]   My comrades so famish'd and queer [unison chorus]
    [Air: O'Carrol]   * Oh the moment was sad ["Savourneen Deelish"]
    [Chos: soldiers]   War, war, war has still its melody [SATB]

Act 2
    [Duet: Madelon, La Gloire]   * + Cou'd you to battle march away
    [Air: Madelon]   * + Little thinks the townsman's wife ["D'un boquet de Romain"]
    [Air: Madelon]   * + I tremble to think that my soldier so bold
    [Chos: inhabitants of Calais]   Sound, sound the solemn strains and slow [SSATB]
    [Glee: inhabitants of Calais]   + Peace to the heroes [SATB]

Act 3
[Air: O'Carrol] * When I was at home ["The Irish washerwoman"]
[Chos: soldiers] Rear our English banner high [SATB]

The libretto is notably theatrical, focusing on Edward III's attempt to starve a French community into submission. Colman forcibly concentrates on the brutalizing effects of ransom and the sanctity of self-sacrifice and forgiveness. The proportion of chorus to aria is far greater than the norm of the period. Flutes and fifes, trumpets, and kettledrums participate in the overture and "military" numbers. The work remained popular for thirty years.

Starred items were published separately (Hoskins, *Arnold*, 2:178-83; RISM A2374-94, also AA2376a-85a). Both **B11** and **B12** were published as op. 33. Crossed items are manuscript copies found in the British Library, Add. Ms. 25014, ff. 8v-10v, and the Royal College of Music, Ms. 2109, ff. 1-4. A copy of the authorized printed libretto (London: Longman, Hurst, Rees, and Orme, 1808) is in the Bodleian Library: M.Adds.III.f.126(1); a copy of the printed song-words (London: Cadell and Davies, 1791) is in the British Library: 11778.f.10; Larpent Ms. 913. For Shakespearean derivations, see Barry Sutcliffe, ed., *Plays by George Colman the Younger and Thomas Morton* (Cambridge: Cambridge University Press, 1983), 29.

B13 **THE ENCHANTED WOOD**
Legendary drama in 3 acts
Libretto by William Bodley Francis (after William Shakespeare's *A Midsummer Night's Dream* and Thomas Parnell's narrative poem "A Fairy Tale," 1721)
First performed at the Haymarket Little Theatre, 25 July 1792
Printed keyboard-vocal score (London: G. Smart, 13 August 1792, as op. 35; RISM A2241)
Singing characters: Ætheria (Mary Taylor), Transit (Maria Bland), Sylphina (Maria DeCamp); Pytheon (Charles Bannister), Owen (John Bannister); chorus of fairies (mixed children's and adult's voices)

B13.1 Overture

II. Andante 3/4, D
III. Allegro 6/8, D

B13.2 Opening solo and chorus (act 1): Ætheria, fairies

A Thematic Index

B13.3 Closing ballet for fairies (act 1)

II. Andante 2/4, B♭
III. [Tempo unmarked] 2/4, C ["Baa baa black sheep"]
IV. [Tempo unmarked] 6/8, B♭ ["Country Dance"]

B13.4 Opening trio (act 2): Owen, Transit, Sylphina

B13.5 Opening duet (act 3): Sylphina, Transit

Text incipits:

Act 1
[Air & Chos: Ætheria, fairies]	Here quickly strike the strings [unison chorus]
[Duet & Chos: Transit Pytheon, fairies]	You that join our mighty trade [chorus: 2 trebles and lower voices]
[Duet: Transit, Sylphina]	Mortal, mortal, mortal man
[Air: Transit]	Wou'd you know how you must find it
[Duet & Chos: Sylphina, Ætheria, fairies]	Sulky pride dare not here venture [unison chorus]

Act 2
[Trio: Owen, Transit, Sylphina]		O when the liquor I do quaff
[Air: Transit]	*	O let me in those ringlets stray
[Air: Pytheon]		My father Pan when I was born
[Air: Owen]		My wife in rage will rattle ["The ram of Derby"]

Act 3
[Duet: Sylphina, Transit]	Hear, Julian, hear
[Fnle: Ætheria, Sylphina, Transit, fairies]	Under elms umbrageous lying [unison chorus]

The plot of this hybrid concerns Julian, a hunchback whose virtue wins the heart of Una; through the magic of Orion (Oberon) Julian loses his deformity. The subplot involves two troublesome verse-speaking fairies (Transit and Sylphina), who play tricks on prose-speaking Owen (Bottom). The innovative tendencies of the score are reflected in the fusion of chorus, ballet, and song. The use of children's voices in the choruses could effectively be associated with the supernatural. Busy string writing is apparent in the overture and what can be anticipated as romantic color is provided by the use of the horn in the second movement. Surprisingly, this work had a short run of six performances.

The starred item was published separately (RISM A2242). A copy of the printed libretto (London: J. Debrett, 1792) is in the Bodleian Library: Vet.A5e.2638; Larpent Ms. 954.

This work as an adaptation of *A Midsummer Night's Dream* is discussed by Mary Anna Blackstone in "The Eighth Fairy: Stage Music and *A Midsummer Night's Dream* to 1800" (Ph.D. diss., University of New Brunswick, 1977).

B14 **THE MOUNTAINEERS**
Play in 3 acts
Libretto by George Colman, the younger (after Miguel de Cervantes, *Don Quixote*, 1605, and William Hodson, *Zoraida*, 1780)
First performed at the Haymarket Little Theatre, 3 August 1793
Printed keyboard-vocal score (London: Preston & Son, 3 September 1793; RISM A2292)
Printed flute score (London: Preston & Son, 1793; RISM A2294)
Singing characters: Zorayda (Elizabeth Kemble), Agnes (Maria Bland); Sadi (John Bannister), Kilmallock (John Johnstone); Muleteers (Charles Bannister, William Davies, George Bland); chorus of Moorish soldiers; goatherds

B14.1 Overture

II. Vivace 3/8, G
III. March 4/4, D

B14.2 Zorayda in the tower [pizzicato strings]

B14.3 Opening song (act 1): Zorayda

B14.4 Moorish march (act 1)

B14.5 Opening glee (act 2): muleteers

B14.6 Opening duet (act 3): Agnes

Text incipits:
Act 1
[Air: Zorayda]   * +Bewailing, bewailing she sunk
[Air: Agnes]   * +When the hollow drum
[Duet: Sadi, Agnes]   * O happy tawny Moor
[Chos: Moorish soldiers]   * The sun is sunk [ATB?]

Act 2
[Glee: muleteers]   * You high-born Spanish noblemen [three voices]
[Air: Kilmallock]   * At sixteen years old ["O dear, what can the matter be?"]
[Chos: goatherds]   Brother goatherd mark you me? [two voices]

Act 3
[Duet: Agnes, Sadi]   * +Faint and wearily the way-worn traveller
[Air: Sadi]   * Think your tawny Moor is true
[Chos: goatherds]   As we goatherds trudge along [unison]

This immensely popular hybrid was written in blank verse and tells how Count Virolet, a slave in Granada, wins the love of a Moorish girl, Zorayda; they escape together. Kemble played the love-mad hermit, Octavion ("The impression which he made was profound," *Morning Chronicle*, 5 August 1793). The plot comes from two intertwined stories in *Don Quixote* (Cardenio's tale, part 1, chapters 27 and 28; and the story of Zoraida, an Algerian maid who becomes a Christian and elopes with her lover, part 1, chapters 40 and 41).

Of particular interest is the beginning of the overture where a solo trumpet signal is answered by a roll of kettledrums. Haydn made the same stylistic point in his "Military" Symphony (no. 100) as here did Arnold. "Oh happy tawny Moor" is accompanied by pizzicato strings representing a guitar. Several versions of "O dear, what can the matter be?" were published during the 1790s.

Starred items were published separately (Hoskins, *Arnold*, 2:189-95; RISM A2295-2313, also AA2295a-2313a). Crossed items are manuscript copies found in the National Library of Wales: Egsair 13, ff. 42v-45v. An unchanged reissue of the piano-keyboard score was published by J. Dale, ca. 1802 (RISM A2293).

Copies of the authorized printed libretto (London: J. Debrett, 1795) and the printed song-words (London: T. Cadell, 1793) are in the British Library: 643.f.3(2); 643.h.14(9); Larpent Ms. 989.

B15   **ZORINSKI**
Play in 3 acts
Libretto by Thomas Morton (after Henry Brooke, *Gustavus Vasa*, 1739)
First performed at the Haymarket Little Theatre, 20 June 1795
Printed keyboard-vocal score (London: Preston & Son, 3 July 1795, as op. 37; RISM A2400)
Printed flute score (London: Preston & Son, 1795; RISM A2401)
Singing characters: Rachel (Elizabeth Leak), Winifred (Maria Bland); O'Curragh (John Johnstone), Zarno (John Bannister), Witski (John Fawcett); chorus of peasants; assassins; soldiers

B15.1 * Overture

II. Polonaise: Vivace 3/4, D

B15.2   Opening chorus (act 1): peasants

B15.3   Opening song (act 2): Zarno

B15.4   Opening song (act 3): Winifred

Text incipits:
Act 1
  [Chos: peasants]   Hail! mighty King [SATB]
  [Air: Rachel]   * Courteous stranger
  [Air: O'Curragh]   * In the dead of the night
  [Duet: Rachel, Zarno]   * When first this little heart began [Charles Dibdin (new)]

Act 2
  [Air: Zarno]   Goodbye my fellow devils dear
  [Duet: Winifred, Witski]   * A piper o'er the meadows straying ["Nos galan"]
  [Qnt: Witski, Winifred,   No longer a ninny
      Zarno, Rachel, O'Curragh]
  [Air: Rachel]   'Twas on a pleasant summer's morn
  [Chos: assassins]   While the hideous night is scowling [ATB]

Act 3
  [Air: Winifred]   Than envied monarchs happier still ["Donald"]
  [Chos: soldiers]   Let the loud ratt'ling drum [SATB]

The basic idea behind this hybrid—that of the patriotism of the Polish people—is expressed in lengthy choruses. The opening chorus of peasants is Handelian in style, while the one for assassins, with its concentration on images of nature, such as the prowling bear and dismal forest, reveals the romantic strain in Arnold's imagination. The second movement of the overture and Rachel's first song are ostensibly polonaises; in the overture finale, solos for violin and oboe occur in alternation.

"In the dead of the night" was originally composed by Arnold for the Vocal Concerts at Willis's Rooms in 1793, when it was sung by "Master Knyvett" (Hoskins, *Arnold*, 2:400). Arnold then included it as an incidental song for Lady Contest in Elizabeth Inchbald's play *The Wedding Day* (F7), and finally in the present opera. Several versions of the Scottish song "Donald" were published during the 1780s.

Starred items were published separately (Hoskins, *Arnold*, 2:217-20; RISM A2402-08, also AA2401a-05c). A copy of the printed libretto (London: T. N. Longman, 1795) is in the Bodleian Library: Malone.B.49(7); Larpent Ms. 1081. See Truth (pseud.), *Mr. Morton's Zorinski and Brooke's Gustavus Vasa Compared, also a Critique on Zorinski . . . with Alterations and Additions* (London, 1795).

B16   **THE ITALIAN MONK**
Play in 3 acts
Libretto by James Boaden (after Ann Radcliffe, *The Italian*, 1797)
First performed at the Haymarket Little Theatre, 15 August 1797
Printed keyboard-vocal score (London: author, 24 August 1797, as op. 43; RISM A2282)
Singing characters: Fioresca (Maria Bland); Carlo (? Trueman), Paullo (Richard Suett); chorus of nuns

B16.1 Overture

Allegro moderato

    II. Chaconne: Andante 3/8, E♭
    III. Rondo [tempo lacking] 2/4, E♭

B16.2 Fioresca's song (act 1)

Vivace

O - ther maid - ens bait their hooks

B16.3 Chorus of nuns (act 1): [women's voices: SS]

[Tempo unmarked]

How calm her life

B16.4 Fioresca's song (act 2):

Larghetto

Dark was the night

B16.5 Trio (act 3): Fioresca, Carlo, Paullo

[Tempo unmarked]

Fioresca: Love no toil re - gard - ing

The *Morning Chronicle*, 18 August 1797, tells us that the drama augmented the stock of gothic theatricals ("a most forcible appeal to the passions"), but Arnold's music is rudimentary. The opening of the overture's finale is played by solo horns and somewhat resembles the second theme from the first movement of Arnold's *Six Overtures*, op. 8, no. 2.

The printed libretto (London: G. G. and J. Robinson, 1797) is in the Bodleian Library: M.Adds. 108d.23, and an edition of the song-words (London: Cadell and Davies, 1797), is in the Alderman Library, University of Virginia. **B16** and **B18** were popular for two or three seasons after their initial production; they belong to the gothicism of the 1790s and the history of melodrama.

B17 CAMBRO-BRITONS

Historical play in 3 acts
Libretto by James Boaden
First performed at the Haymarket Little Theatre, 21 July 1798
Printed keyboard-vocal score (London: Longman & Broderip, 18 August 1798, as op. 45; RISM A2219)
Singing characters: Winifred (Maria Bland); O'Turloch (John Johnstone), Gwyn (Richard Suett); chorus of angels; Welsh bards; peasants

B17.1 Overture

II. Andante 3/4, G [2 harps]
III. Andante 6/8, G [harp and union pipes]
IV. Rondo: Allegro 2/4, D [2 harps]

B17.2 Opening song (act 1): Winifred [flute, harp, triangle, tambourine]

B17.3 Opening song (act 2): O'Turloch

B17.4 Opening song (act 3): Winifred

B17.5 March (act 3) [piccolo, bassoons, trumpet, timpani, strings]

Text incipits:
Act 1
  [Air: Winifred]   When the rude voice of war I no longer shall hear
  [Air: O'Turloch]   When I was a boy ["Irish melody"]

Act 2
  [Air: O'Turloch]   To win all the fair ones
  [Trio: O'Turloch, Winifred,   King Arthur kept at merry Carlisle [2 harps]
    Gwyn]
  [Chos: angels]   Dear is the incense that repentance flings [SS; flutes and bassoon]

Act 3
  [Air: Winifred]   The sun was set, the night was grey
  [Chos: bards]   Ruin seize thee, ruthless king [ATB?; harps, cello]
  [Chos: peasants]   Hither from our cloud top't mountains [SATB]

The action is set during the invasion of Wales by Edward I, and revolves around two Welsh patriot brothers who are rivals in love. The national element is musically stressed by choruses and instrumentation (harps and union pipes). The overture and chorus of bards contain extensive harp arpeggiation.

A copy of the printed libretto (London: G. G. and J. Robinson, 1798) is in the British Library: 161.g.47; a copy of the printed song-words (London: Cadell and Davies, 1798) is in the Bodleian Library: Vet.A5e.2401; Larpent Ms. 1222. George Colman, the younger, wrote the words for two songs.

B18 FALSE AND TRUE (THE IRISHMAN IN ITALY)
Play in 3 acts
Libretto by George Moultrie
First performed at the Haymarket Little Theatre, 11 August 1798
Printed keyboard-vocal score (London: author, 25 August 1798, as op. 46; RISM A2245)
Singing characters: Lauretta (Miss Griffiths), Janetta (Maria Bland); Nicolo (? D'Arcy), Tomaso (George Davenport), Benini (Joseph Munden), O'Rafarty (John Johnstone), Count Florenzi (? Trueman); masqueraders (un-named); chorus of revellers

B18.1 Overture

II. Vivace 2/4, C

B18.2 Opening trio (act 1): masqueraders

B18.3 Opening song (act 2): Janetta

B18.4 Opening song (act 3): O'Rafarty

B18.5 Dance (act 3): "Moll i'th wad"

Text incipits:
Act 1
  [Trio: masqueraders]   When you discover [SSB?]
  [Air: Lauretta]   When alas my true love left me
  [Trio: Lauretta, Nicolo,   Ah how delighted will she be
     Tomaso]

Act 2
  [Air: Janetta]   When miss's lover's call'd away
  [Duet: Janetta, Benini]   I ne'er knew a lady
  [Air: O'Rafarty]   Old father McShane [John Johnstone (new)]
  [Air: Lauretta]   On our green tambourine ["Italian air"]
  [Air: Janetta]   Lorenza rich and high in power
  [Duet: Janetta, Nicolo]   From this happy day

Act 3
  [Air: O'Rafarty]   The sweet kiss of my dear
  [Solo & Chos: Benini,   Tho' years glide away [unison chorus]
     revellers]
  [Fnle: Lauretta, Janetta,   Let the swell of harmony [SATB chorus]
     Florenzi; chorus of
     revellers]

This pseudo-gothic hybrid pivots on Juliana, who is betrothed to Count Florenzi. Marchese Caliari, enamored of Juliana and spurred on by jealousy, twice contrives to murder Florenzi before he is banished. A copy of the printed libretto (London: J. Bell, 1798) is in the Bodleian Library: Vet.A5e.2009(5); Larpent Ms. 1223.

Cues for solo flute as well as oboes and trumpets occur in the overture and the instrumentation of the opening waltz (flutes and percussion) is reminiscent of its counterpart in *Cambro-Britons* (**B17**). A cello solo opens Lauretta's first song.

C / *Afterpiece Operas with Spoken Dialogue*

C1 **THE MADMAN**
Pasticcio burletta in 1 act; music not extant
Librettist possibly D. J. Piguenit
First performed at Marylebone Gardens, 28 August 1770

From an advertisement in the *Public Advertiser* of 27 August 1770, we learn that this work was a pastiche compiled by Arnold with borrowings from Thomas Arne, Charles Burney, Charles Dibdin, Niccolò Piccini, and Mattia Vento. The plot revolves around a charade wherein Lovemore masquerades as a doctor and consigns Emily's lecherous old guardian to a madhouse. In act 1 the departing hero sings "Water parted" from Arne's *Artaxerxes* (1762) and with the original words. A copy of the printed libretto (London: C. D. Piguenit, 1770) is in the British Library: 644.k.19(12); libretto reveals 14 vocal numbers, lost; also overture.

C2 **LILLIPUT**
Musical entertainment in 1 act; revival with new music by Arnold
Libretto by David Garrick revised by George Colman, the elder (after the first part of Jonathan Swift's *Gulliver's Travels*, 1726)
First performed at the Haymarket Little Theatre, 15 May 1777
Printed keyboard-vocal score (London: John Johnston, ca. 1777; RISM A2283)

    C2.1   Overture ["Boys and girls come out to play"]

    C2.2   Song: Lady Flimnap

    C2.3   The Procession

    C2.4   Lilliputian Catch (3 voices)

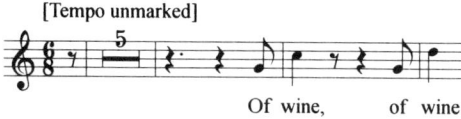

C2.5   Lillputian Pageant

"March"

I. "The Garland" Allegro 2/4, G
II. "March for Gulliver" 4/4, D
III. "The Ostrich" Minuetto 3/4, G

George Colman began his management of the Haymarket Little Theatre by reviving Garrick's *Lilliput* (1756). For this production Colman devised a "Grand Jubilee Pageant, in Honour of Gulliver" with processional music by Arnold. The instrumental writing, scored for strings on three staves, is extremely simple, melodically and rhythmically. The stately minuet, written to accompany "a lady with a tête stuck full of feathers, riding on an ostrich with a bare rump" (*Morning Chronicle*, 16 May 1777) lampoons fashion and novelty. The overture follows the continental fashion for one movement, but this genre never got much of a foothold in the English playhouse. The text of this revision does not survive. Lillian Gottesman, in "Garrick's *Lilliput*," *Restoration and Eighteenth Century Theatre Research* 11, no. 2 (1972): 34-37, offers a brief account of the 1756 entertainment.

C3   **THE GIPSIES**
Comic opera in 2 acts; music not extant
Libretto by Charles Dibdin (after Charles-Simon Favart, *La Bohémienne*, 1755)
First performed at the Haymarket Little Theatre, 3 August 1778

The story of the prince in disguise finding true love among the peasants is a recurring one throughout the eighteenth century, but general opinion judged that *The Gipsies* was just absurd. Arnold's music was described as "middling" (*Morning Chronicle*, 4 August 1778). The piece ran for six nights. A copy of the printed libretto (London: T. Cadell, 1778) is in the British Library: 161.e.31; libretto reveals 13 vocal numbers, lost; also overture.

C4   **THE SON-IN-LAW**
Comic opera in 2 acts
Libretto by John O'Keeffe
First performed at the Haymarket Little Theatre, 14 August 1779
Printed keyboard-vocal score (London: J. Blundell, ca. 1780, as op. 14; RISM A2343)
Parallel keyboard edition (London: J. Preston, ca. 1782; RISM A2344)
"Piano-Forte Magazine" edition (London: Harrison, Cluse & Co., as vol. 7, no. 9, ca. 1799; RISM A2345)
Singing characters: Cecilia (Elizabeth Harper); Bouquet (Charles Wood), Bowkitt (John Edwin), Cranky (William Parsons), Signor Arionelli (Charles Bannister)

C / Afterpiece Operas with Spoken Dialogue

C4.1 Overture

II. Rondo: Allegro 2/4, B♭

C4.2 Opening song (act 1): Cecilia

C4.3 Opening song (act 2): Cranky

Text incipits:
Act 1
[Air: Cecilia]	*	Tho' sweetly breathes the smiling spring
[Air: Cranky]	*	Maidens do not think me stupid [François Philidor]
[Air: Bouquet]	*	This face observe discerning fair [Nicolas Dezède, "Lison dormait," *Julie* (1772)]
[Air: Bowkitt]		With an air debonair[†]
[Trio: Bowkitt, Bouquet, Cecilia]		You're so charming and fair

Act 2
[Air: Cranky]		I like the plain song ["Lango lee"]
[Aria: Cecilia]	*	Goddess of the magic cestus [solo oboe and bassoon; strings]
[Recit.: Sig. Arionelli]		In gratitude to thy exalted friendship
[Aria: Sig. Arionelli]		Water parted from the sea [Thomas Arne, *Artaxerxes* (1762)]
[Air: Sig. Arionelli]	*	Signor Cranky then addio [Pietro Guglielmi]
[Fnle: Cranky, Cecilia, Bouquet]		No longer Cupid's foe

O'Keeffe's text is a satirical exposure of fashion and pseudo-refinement and Arnold's music occasionally achieves burlesque effects as in Bowkitt's "With an air debonair," with its parody minuet and country dance. Cecilia's "Goddess of the magic cestus" is modelled on *seria* convention. In the rondo finale of the overture, solo oboe and bassoon introduce the main theme each time it recurs. In the story, Cecilia's father keeps mistaking the identity of his future son-in-law.

[†] The source of the title of Susan L. Porter's book *With an Air Debonair: Musical Theatre in America, 1785-1815* (Washington: Smithsonian Institution Press, 1991).

Starred items were published separately (Hoskins, *Arnold*, 2:82-84; RISM A2346-51); A2343 is reprinted in Link, *O'Keeffe*, 1. A copy of the unauthorized printed libretto (Dublin: booksellers, 1781) is in the Bodleian Library: Vet.A5f.670(3); also a copy of the printed song-words (London: anon., 1781): Douce S134(13). The earliest authentic text is that in *Cumberland's British Theatre* 31, British Library copy: 642.a.16; Larpent Ms. 489. *The London Stage* lists *The Son-in-Law* as fourth in frequency of performance among afterpieces produced 1776-1800.

C5   **FIRE AND WATER**
Comic opera in 2 acts; music mostly not extant
Libretto by Miles Peter Andrews
First performed at the Haymarket Little Theatre, 8 July 1780

C5.1   Song (act 1): Nancy ["French air"; RISM A2247]

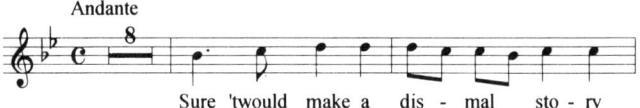

C5.2   Song (act 1): Ambuscade [RISM A2246]

The scene is set at Portsmouth where a French invasion is expected, and the action deals with the attempt of three incendiaries to destroy the dockyards. This work was a one-season success, but reviewers hardly noticed Arnold's score. From newspaper advertisements we learn the overture was, appropriately, a medley "selected from the Fire and Water Music of Handel" (*Morning Chronicle*, July 8). Ambuscade's surviving song is also a medley, including Handel's "See, the conqu'ring hero comes" from *Judas Maccabaeus* (1746), Dibdin's "Blow high, blow low" from *The Seraglio* (1776), and Arnold's own "If 'tis joy to wound a lover" from *Rosamond* (**A1**). Nancy's extant song is apparently French. It appears from textual sources that the opera opened with a chorus of dockyarders, while act 1 ended in a "Song and Chorus by Handel."

Copies of the printed song-words and libretto (both London: T. Cadell, 1780) are in the British Library: 11777.c.38; 161.g.5; Larpent Ms. 522; printed libretto reveals 13 vocal numbers, lost; also overture.

C6   **THE WEDDING NIGHT**
Musical farce in 1 act; music not extant
Libretto by James Cobb
First performed at the Haymarket Little Theatre, 12 August 1780

C / Afterpiece Operas with Spoken Dialogue

According to the *Gazetteer*, 14 August 1780, Arnold's score included a medley overture and several songs to existing melodies. The song-words in the libretto (Larpent Ms. 530) indicate a "grammatical" song sung by a schoolmaster, and this anticipates a similar one by Lingo in *The Agreeable Surprise* (**C10**); libretto reveals 10 vocal numbers, lost; also overture. The story tells of newlyweds who are plagued by visitors on their wedding night.

C7   **THE DEAD ALIVE**
Comic opera in 2 acts
Libretto by John O'Keeffe (after "Aben Hassam and his wife" from *Arabian Nights' Entertainments*)
First performed at the Haymarket Little Theatre, 16 June 1781
Printed keyboard-vocal score (London: Longman & Broderip, 1781, as op. 18; copy in the Library of Congress: ML50.6.D3A7)
Singing characters: Caroline (Elizabeth Harper), Comfit (Sarah Wilson), Miss Wintertop (Lydia Webb); Edward (Charles Wood), Sir Walter Weathercock (Richard Wilson)

C7.1   Overture

II. Adagio 4/4, B♭
III. Rondo: Vivace 2/4, B♭

C7.2   Opening song (act 1): Edward

C7.3   Opening song (act 2): Motley

Text incipits:
Act 1
  [Air: Edward]   If balmy friendship yet survives
  [Air: Caroline]   While pert cock sparrows sport and play
  [Duet: Edward, Caroline] Let me but my Caroline guard

A THEMATIC INDEX

[Air: Comfit]	When I left Primrose Green
[Air: Motley]	An actor's a comical dog
[Air: Caroline]	See the blossom of spring [Thomas Arne, "Thou soft flowing Avon," *An Ode upon Dedicating a Building to Shakespeare* (1769)]
[Duet: Miss Wintertop, Sir Walter]	Away sir, get out of my sight

Act 2
[Air: Motley]	The world is all nonsense and noise
[Duet: Sir Walter, Miss Wintertop]	In vain to smother love we strive
[Air: Motley]	* See a nymph so brisk and witty ["Twinkum twankum"]
[Fnle: Sir Walter, Miss Wintertop, Edward, Caroline, Motley, Comfit]	Then away with all care

The plot pivots on Edward and Caroline who, having married against relatives' wishes, lose their respective inheritances. To win their way out of poverty, each fakes the death of the other. The opening solos of Edward and Caroline adopt the same key succession and in the following duet, when flutes join the strings, their voices blend in sixths and thirds. In all Motley's songs an Irish folk origin seems certain; they are tunes O'Keeffe probably sang to Arnold. Oboe, bassoon, and horn solos occur in the rondo finale of the overture.

The starred item was published separately (RISM A2240). A copy of the printed libretto (unauthorized edition, Dublin: booksellers, 1783) is in the Bodleian Library: Vet.A5f.1109(9); Larpent Ms. 559.

C8 THE SILVER TANKARD (THE POINT AT PORTSMOUTH)
Comic opera in 2 acts; music not extant
Libretto by Elizabeth, Baroness Craven, later Margravine of Anspach
First performed at the Haymarket Little Theatre, 18 July 1781

This work had a short run of six performances; the *Morning Herald* of 19 July 1781 disregarded it as "a tiresome procession of sing-song." According to the published song-words (London: T. Cadell, 1781; copy in Harvard University Library: EC8.C8553.781a), there were 17 vocal numbers: a third of the music was by Arnold and borrowings were drawn from Thomas Arne, William Boyce, Charles Burney, and Tommaso Giordani, as well as English and French ballads. Amongst Arnold's settings were two interesting texts—an old Lancashire ballad ("With arms across, along the strand") and part of John Suckling's song "Honest lover whosoever" ("If fondly thou dost not mistake"). Arnold's overture was apparently a medley of popular sea-songs (*Morning Chronicle*, 19 July 1781). Larpent Ms. 564. The title refers to an heirloom which Nancy gives to her sailor-lover in the hope of retrieving his fortunes.

C9 HODGE-PODGE (A RECEIPT TO MAKE A BENEFIT)
Musical farce in 1 act; music not extant
Libretto by George Colman, the elder
First performed at the Haymarket Little Theatre, 28 August 1781

According to the *Morning Chronicle* of 28 August 1781, this piece was a successful satire on medley-entertainments. The music included Arnold's "sneezing" trio-finale to act 1 of *The Spanish Barber* (**B2**); also Daniel Purcell's "Mad Bess" from *The Pilgrim* (1698), Thomas Arne's "Sweet echo" from *Comus* (1738), and William Boyce's "With horns and with hounds" from *The Secular Masque* (1750). Arnold has been credited with this composition; see the *Monthly Mirror* 10 (March 1803): 228. The libretto does not survive.

C10 **THE AGREEABLE SURPRISE (THE SECRET ENLARGED)**
Comic opera in 2 acts
Libretto by John O'Keeffe
First performed at the Haymarket Little Theatre, 4 September 1781
Printed keyboard-vocal score (London: J. Bland, 6 September 1782, as op. 16; RISM A2194)
Second keyboard edition (London: Harrison & Co., ca. 1782; RISM A2194a)
"Piano-Forte Magazine" edition (London: Harrison, Cluse & Co., as vol. 1, no. 1, ca. 1799; RISM A2195)
Printed flute score (London: J. Bland, 1782; RISM A2195)
Singing characters: Laura (Elizabeth Harper), Mrs. Cheshire (Lydia Webb), Cowslip (Mary Wells); Sir Felix Friendly (Richard Wilson), Compton (Charles Bannister), Lingo (John Edwin), Eugene (Charles Wood); chorus of harvesters

C10.1   Overture

II. Minuetto affettuoso 3/4, G

C10.2   Opening chorus (act 1): harvesters

C10.3   Opening song (act 2): Sir Felix

Text incipits:
Act 1
  [Chos & solos: harvesters,   Here we sing, dance and play [unison chorus]
   Compton, Sir Felix]

[Air: Compton]	* Thus my boys, our anchor's weigh'd
[Air: Compton]	The virgin lily of the night
[Air: Sir Felix]	* In Jacky Bull [English tune]
[Aria: Laura]	* The tuneful lark [flute, piccolo, strings]
[Air: Lingo]	* Such beauties in view [Irish tune]
[Qnt: Sir Felix, Compton, Eugene, Laura, Lingo]	Oh how sweetly pleasure's tasted

Act 2

[Air: Sir Felix]	* Some like great bowls to quaff
[Air: Mrs. Cheshire]	* In choice of a husband
[Air: Lingo]	* Amo, amas, I love a lass ["The mouse and the frog"]
[Air: Cowslip]	* Lord, what care I for mam and dad? ["Corn-rigs are bonny"]
[Air: Lingo]	* Of all the pretty flowers [Irish tune]
[Air: Laura]	Ah, why take back the vows you gave
[Air: Eugene]	* My Laura, wilt thou trust the seas
[Fnle: Sir Felix, Laura, Eugene, Mrs. Cheshire, Compton, Lingo]	A kiss my girl, your hand my boy

The story of children swapped at birth and the resulting complexities in adulthood is farce at O'Keeffe's best, especially in the characters of Cowslip the dairymaid, Mrs. Cheshire the cheesemonger, and Lingo the schoolmaster-turned-butler. Tuneful strophic airs are appropriate in the representation of comic country characters, and Arnold's score has some good examples. The folksong borrowings are often employed for purposes of parody, and the Irish examples were probably drawn from O'Keeffe's own memories (O'Keeffe, *Recollections*, 2:5-6; see also 3-4). Lingo's "Amo, amas" is still sung. In Laura's coloratura aria, solo flute and piccolo imitate birdsong. This work was popular for thirty years: *The London Stage* lists it as third among afterpieces most frequently produced 1776-1800.

Starred items were published separately (see Hoskins, *Arnold*, 2:98-101; RISM A2196-2202, also AA2196a-2202a); A2194 is reprinted in Link, *O'Keeffe*, 1. Copies of printed song-words (London: T. Cadell, 1781) and libretto (London: T. Cadell, 1784) are in the British Library: 11777.c.6; 11777.a.55; Larpent Ms. 568.

C11 NONE ARE SO BLIND AS THOSE WHO WON'T SEE
Musical farce in 2 acts; music not extant
Libretto by Charles Dibdin (after Louis-François Dorvigny's unpublished *L'Aveugle prétendu*)
First performed at the Haymarket Little Theatre, 2 July 1782

In 1782 Charles Dibdin, in debt and out of work, sent Arnold this libretto, which the composer set out of compassion. According to the *Morning Chronicle* of July 3, the piece was "a mere exhibition of farcical characters" with "music, which is for the most part very pretty, the overture especially." What the audience came for was Ralph Wewitzer's performance of Dr. Caterpillar, a satire on a celebrated quack philosopher of the day called Katterfelto. This work had a short run of six performances. Larpent Ms. 594.

C / AFTERPIECE OPERAS WITH SPOKEN DIALOGUE

C12 **THE FEMALE DRAMATIST**
Musical farce in 2 acts; music not extant
Libretto by George Colman, the elder (after Mr. Melopoyn's story in Tobias Smollett's *Roderick Random*, 1748, chapters 62-63)
First performed at the Haymarket Little Theatre, 16 August 1782

This piece was indifferently received by critics for the *Morning Chronicle*, 17 August 1782, and the *London Chronicle*, 15-17 August 1782. The words for five songs and a chorus are printed in the *London Chronicle*, 15-17 August 1782; John Edwin's "What is a poet, sir?" is set to the tune "I went to Abingdon." The music is credited to Arnold in the *Monthly Mirror* 10 (March 1803): 228. Mrs. Metaphone, the "female dramatist," is based on Mr. Melopoyn, a playwright in Smollett's *Roderick Random* who tries to get his tragedy accepted for the stage.

C13 **THE BIRTH DAY (THE PRINCE OF ARRAGON)**
An opera in 2 acts
Libretto by John O'Keeffe (after George-François Saint-Foix's *Le Rival supposé*, 1749)
First performed at the Haymarket Little Theatre, 12 August 1783
Printed keyboard-vocal score (London: author, 1 September 1783, as op. 21; RISM A2217)
Singing characters: Florina (Georgina George), Seraphina (Elizabeth Bannister); Don Leopold (Richard Wilson)

C13.1   Overture

II. Minuetto 3/4, D

C13.2   Opening song (act 1): Don Leopold

C13.3   Opening song (act 1): Florina

Text incipits:

Act 1
[Air: Don Leopold]		A court is the fountain of honour
[Air: Florina]	*	Your wise men all declare
[Air: Seraphina]		Sweetest passion of the mind
[Air: Seraphina]		My dawn of life
[Duet: Seraphina, Florina]		Sweet content can banish strife

Act 2
- [Air: Florina] — Quick for a smile implore me [Niccolò Piccini]
- [Air: Don Leopold] — When first an Arragonian maid
- [Air: Seraphina] — Ah, fond lover, soothe my anguish [Niccolò Piccini, "E pur bella," *La buona figliuola maritata* (1761)]
- [Fnle: Don Leopold, Seraphina, Florina] — Hail, happy people now rejoice

This pseudo-pastoral piece was written to celebrate the Prince of Wales's twenty-first birthday, and Arnold's music was an apt response to the festive situation; the score is dedicated to "His Royal Highness." By far the most popular item was Florina's first song, which was published separately in full score (two oboes, two horns, and strings) in 1787 under the title "The Je ne sçai quois" (RISM A2339)—the item is a textual parody on "The Je ne sçai quois" by William Whitehead (1715-85). This publication occurred after Arnold incorporated the ballad in *The Siege of Curzola* (**B8**). A copy of the libretto (London: T. Cadell, 1783) is in the British Library: 11777.c.67; Larpent Ms. 628.

C14 **GRETNA GREEN**
Pasticcio comic opera in 2 acts
Libretto by Charles Stuart, with alterations and song-words by John O'Keeffe
First performed at the Haymarket Little Theatre, 28 August 1783
Printed keyboard-vocal score (London: J. Preston, 13 September 1783, as op. 22; RISM A2254)
Singing characters: Signora Figurante (Giovanna Sestini), Maria (Elizabeth Bannister), Miss Plumb (Catherine Morris), Lady Pedigree (Lydia Webb); Rory (Richard Wilson), Captain Gorget (Charles Bannister)

C14.1   Overture

II. Affettuoso 3/4, A ["The braes of Ballenden"]; Vivace 2/2, D ["Scotch medley"]

C14.2   Begging Prologue: Rory

The mu-sic's pre-par'd!

C14.3 Opening song (act 1): Rory

I can shoe a horse

C14.4 Opening song (act 2): Rory

I saw a stout fellow ride very queer

Text incipits:
Act 1

[Begging Prologue: Rory]	The music's prepar'd [medley from John Gay and Johann Pepusch, *The Beggar's Opera* (1728)]
[Air: Rory]	I can shoe a horse ["Dainty Davy"]
[Air: Rory]	From fair London city ["Paddy whack"]
[Air: Sgra. Figurante]	Soft Arno's stream ["French air"; oboe and strings]
[Air: Rory]	My bottle is my wife and friend ["Jack-o'-Latin"]
[Air: Maria]	I laugh, I dance, I pipe ["Etrick banks"]
[Air: Maria]	My fond heart sweetly basks ["Banks of the Tweed"]
[Air: Miss Plumb]	See Lady Tonish ["Duraling"]
[Fnle: Rory, Maria, Miss Plumb, Sgra. Figurante]	Blind Cupid's darts ["Low down in the broom"]

Act 2

[Air: Rory]	I saw a stout fellow ["Country bumkin"]
[Aria: Sgra. Figurante]	Away you wild inconstant lover [Tommaso Giordani, *La frascatona* (1776)]
[Air: Maria]	Since that clear day ["Logan water"]
[Air: Gorget]	With honour's scars ["The flowers of Edinburgh"]
[Aria: Gorget]	September the thirteenth
[Aria: Sgra. Figurante]	From branch to branch [Tommaso Giordani (new?)]
[Fnle: Gorget, Maria, Lady Pedigree, Miss Plumb, Sgra. Figurante, Rory]	Secure in my Maria's heart ["Old highland laddie"]

Arnold's "Begging Prologue," built out of tunes from *The Beggar's Opera*, readily identifies this work with the ballad opera genre and its prototype. The plot pivots around an elopement to Gretna Green and, appropriately, the majority of the borrowings are from Scottish folksong. Arnold's only vocal item is a full-scale aria intended to commemorate Elliot's decisive victory at Gibraltar on 13 September 1782, and the middle section describes a raging battle at sea (there is a manuscript copy in Glasgow University Library: Bi 22z.29, pp. 220-21). The second movement of the overture opens with an oboe solo. A copy of the printed libretto (unauthorized; Dublin, [1783]) is in the Bodleian Library: Vet.A5f.1650; Larpent Ms. 634.

C15 HUNT THE SLIPPER

Musical farce in 2 acts
Libretto by Henry Knapp (after a French comedy of the same name)
First performed at the Haymarket Little Theatre, 21 August 1784
Printed keyboard-vocal score (London: for the author by Harrison & Co., 23 September 1784, as op. 21; RISM A2260)

C15.1   Song (act 1): Billy Bristle

B15.2   Song 2 (act 1): Billy Bristle

B15.3   Song 3 (act 1): Winterbottom

B15.4   Song 4 (act 2): Billy Bristle

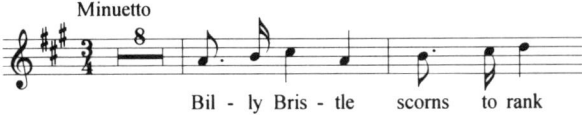

The plot pivots on a love letter which is discovered hidden in a slipper by a maiden aunt. Arnold's songs are in patter-style; in the last, the word "yawn" is set to falling phrases and sustained notes. John Edwin sang the part of Billy Bristle and Richard Wilson the part of Winterbottom. A copy of the unauthorized libretto (Dublin: for the booksellers, 1792), is in the Bodleian Library: Vet.A5f.1852(3). Larpent Ms. 660.

C16 PEEPING TOM

Comic opera in 2 acts
Libretto by John O'Keeffe (after the Lady Godiva legend)
First performed at the Haymarket Little Theatre, 6 September 1784
Printed keyboard-vocal score (London: for the author by Harrison & Co., 13 September 1784; RISM A2317)

"Piano-Forte Magazine" edition (London: Harrison & Co., as vol. 2, no. 3, 1797; British Library copy: D.854; other copies in the Manchester Public Library, Boston Public Library, Harvard University Library, Duke University Library, University of California, William Andrews Clough Memorial Library)

Printed flute score (London: for the author by Harrison & Co., ca. 1784, as nos. 19-20 in the *New Musical Magazine for the German Flute*; RISM AA238a)

Singing characters: Emma (Elizabeth Bannister), Maud (Mary Wells), Mayoress (Lydia Webb); Harold (Charles Bannister), Mayor of Coventry (Richard Wilson), Tom (John Edwin), Crazy (Ralph Wewitzer)

C16.1 * Overture

II. Andante 2/4, C (medley of tunes from the opera)

C16.2   Opening song (act 1): Emma

C16.3   Opening song (act 2): Tom

Text incipits:

Act 1
[Air: Emma]		Glitt'ring trifle sport of fashion
[Air: Harold]		Paphian bowers ["Garron" (Gardom?)]
[Duet: Mayor, Maud]		The deuce o' one ["We go up Holborn Hill"]
[Trio: Tom, Crazy, Mayor]	*	Merry are the bells [Carolan, "Irish lamentation"]
[Air: Maud]		What pleasure to think
[Air: Mayor]		The slender waist
[Air: Tom]	*	Egad, we had a glorious feast
[Duet: Emma, Harold]		Of love, sweet love ["Venetian ballad"]
[Fnle: Mayor, Mayoress, Maud, Tom]		Dear wife forgive ["My father he kiss'd"]

Act 2
[Air: Tom]	Your worship your wings may clap ["Tatter the road"]
[Trio: Tom, Crazy, Mayoress]	Your lordship is welcome ["Rub-a-dub"]
[Air: Emma]	Adieu, dearest friend ["French air"]
[Air: Harold]	The soldier in his calm retreat

[Air: Tom]   When I was a younker ["Kisses and brandy"]
[Fnle: Harold, Emma, Maud,   Let envy, care and tumult cease ["Peggy Benson"]
Mayoress, Mayor, Crazy,
Tom]

This work is of particular interest in that it makes use of modal folk tunes, most of them English—they are identified in the printed song-words (London: T. Cadell, 1785; copy in the Bodleian Library: Vet.A5e.1417C(1)). A special place in the opera is occupied by the "medley" movement of the overture, which is a remarkable example of Arnold's enterprising orchestration: there are cues for piccolo, flute, clarinets, oboe, bassoon, horns, trumpets, kettledrums, and bells (i.e., a glockenspiel in its original form of a miniature carillon with tiny bells played from a keyboard). In Harold's second solo there are cues for fife, trumpets, and timpani. Despite an uninspired text, this work achieved 152 performances over the rest of the century. In 1793, when Jack Bannister took on the title role, Arnold wrote an additional short song, which begins:

C16.4   Moderato

Sir So-lo-mons Si - mons when he did wed

(London: Thomas Skillern for B. Wood, 12 January 1793; RISM A2321)

This item was printed in several editions (RISM A2321-4; also Hoskins, *Arnold*, 2:140-41). The starred items were also published separately (RISM A2319-20; Hoskins, *Arnold*, 2:139-40). A copy of the printed libretto (unauthorized; Dublin: booksellers, 1785) is in the Bodleian Library: Vet.A5f.670(8); Larpent Ms. 662. *The London Stage* lists *Peeping Tom* as sixth in frequency of performance among afterpieces produced 1776-1800.

C17   **THE BASKET MAKER**
Musical piece in 2 acts; music not extant
Libretto by John O'Keeffe
First performed at the Haymarket Little Theatre, 4 September 1790

The story is principally concerned with Simon Rochefort who, temporarily dispossessed of his lands, joins a tribe of Iroquois indians. Arnold's overture was especially liked (*Public Advertiser*, 6 September 1790; *London Chronicle*, September 4-7). Copies of the printed song-words (London: T. Cadell, 1790) and libretto (London: T. Woodfall, 1798) are in the British Library: 11777.c.68;82.d.1; they reveal 8 vocal numbers, lost; also overture.

C18   **THE CHILDREN IN THE WOOD**
Comic opera in 2 acts
Libretto by Thomas Morton (after a French version of the ballad of the same name)
First performed at the Haymarket Little Theatre, 1 October 1793
Printed keyboard-vocal score (London: Longman & Broderip, 17 October 1793, as op. 35; RISM A2228)

Printed flute score (London: Longman & Broderip, 1793; RISM A2229)
Singing characters: Josephine (Maria Bland), Girl (Miss Mary Menage), Lady Helen (Maria DeCamp); Walter (John Bannister), Boy (Master Frederick Menage), Apathy (Richard Suett), Lord Alford (Charles Dignum)

C18.1 * Overture

II. Slow 3/4, D ["Three children skating on the ice"]
III. Vivace 2/4, D

C18.2 Opening song (act 1): Josephine

C18.3 Opening song (act 2): Lady Helen

Text incipits:

Act 1
[Air: Josephine]	*	When love gets you fast in her clutches
[Air: Walter]	*	There was Dorothy Dump
[Duet: Josephine, Boy]	*	Young Simon in his lovely Sue
[Duet: Josephine, Apathy]		Great Sir consider
[Air: Girl]	*	See brother, see on yonder bough [flageolet and strings]

Act 2
[Air: Lady Helen]		Mark the true test of passion
[Air: Lord Alford]	*	When first to Helen's lute ["Ay wakin' oh"]
[Air: Josephine]		A yeoman of no mean degree ["The Ditty"]
[Fnle: Walter, Helen, Alford, Josephine]		Have I sav'd this girl and boy

This work became one of the most popular afterpiece operas of the late eighteenth century, and John Bannister became famous for his role as Walter, the coward-hero who saves the children from their assassins. Arnold's music is remarkable for the structural skill of the overture and for the inclusion of a previously unrecorded example of English folksong ("The Ditty" published subsequently by Ralph Vaughan Williams as "The Truth from Above"). The overture is rich in cues for solo instruments, and in "See brother, see" a flageolet represents birdsong. The maid and butler sing their duet while the master silently flirts with the maid. For a full discussion of this work, see Susan Porter's critical introduction to the facsimile reproduction of the 1793 piano-score and the 1795 American libretto, *Nineteenth-Century American Musical Theater*, vol. 1 (New York: Garland, 1994), and her "Children in the Wood: The Odyssey of an Anglo-American Ballad," in *Vistas of American Music: Essays and Compositions in Honor of William K. Kearns*, ed. Porter and John Graziano (this publisher, 1998); also Barry Sutcliffe's edition in *Plays by George Colman the Younger and Thomas Morton* (Cambridge: Cambridge University Press, 1983).

Starred items were published separately (Hoskins, *Arnold*, 2:198-202; RISM A2230-38, also AA2230a-38a). There is a copy of the printed libretto (London: n.p., 1794) in the British Library: 11777.b.7(6); Larpent Ms. 991.

C19 **AULD ROBIN GRAY**
Pastoral entertainment in 2 acts
Libretto by Samuel James Arnold
First performed at the Haymarket Little Theatre, 26 July 1794
Printed keyboard-vocal score (London: Preston & Son, 8 August 1794, as op. 36; RISM A2203)
Singing characters: Jenny (Elizabeth Leak), Susan (Maria DeCamp), Moggy (Maria Bland), Mother (Ursula Booth); Jerry (John Fawcett), Jemmy (Elizabeth Kemble), Sandy (George Bland), Auld Robin Gray (Richard Suett), Donald (William Davies), Duncan (Thomas Sedgwick); chorus of sailors

C19.1 * Scottish medley overture

C19.2   Opening song (act 1): Jerry

'Twas on Christ-mas day

C19.3 * "A Storm at Sea and Shipwreck-Prelude of Music" (act 2)

C19.4   Opening song (act 2): Duncan

Mark the hue of the li - ly

C19.5   Closing reel (act 2)

[Tempo unmarked]

Text incipits:

Act 1

[Air: Jerry]	*	'Twas on Christmas day ["Dance to your daddy"]
[Air: Jenny]		Oh how could you leave your own Jenny ["Thro' the wood laddie"]
[Duet: Jemmy, Jenny]		'Erst when my lovely Jane ["Auld Robin Gray"]
[Aria: Susan]		How vain is caution
[Air: Moggy]		No lav'rocks e'er so sweetly sung
[Duet: Sandy, Moggy]		Pretty Moggy, cease I pray
[Air: Jenny]		Now my flocks have gone
[Qnt: Jenny, Mother, Susan, Auld Robin, Donald]		Oh the joys of wedded life

Act 2

[Air: Duncan]		Mark the hue of the lily
[Chos: sailors]		Oh, yeo! Oh, yeo! Heave the anchor [ATB]
[Air: Sandy]		I'm a braw and bonny youth
[Air: Jerry]		When I to London first came in
[Duet: Duncan, Susan]	*	When first I saw my Susan's face
[Glee: Moggy, Jerry, Sandy]		Begone vain fool ["Begone dull care" (1793)]
[Fnle: Donald, Moggy, Duncan, Susan, Jerry, Jenny, Auld Robin]		Fate her forms at length redressing ["The Mallow Fling"]

The plot relates how Jenny, believing that her sailor-lover is drowned, reluctantly agrees to marry Auld Robin Gray. Jemmy returns however, with news of sudden fortune and in time to claim his bride. Arnold's new music mainly adopts the traits of Scottish folksong, a notable exception being Susan's aria with parts for solo oboe and bassoon. The storm prelude is borrowed from the "earthquake" ending Haydn's *Seven Last Words* (performed at the Hanover Square Rooms on 13 June 1791 and 3 May 1792). Haydn attended a performance of this opera and disliked it (Landon, *Haydn*, 3:265). Newspaper reviewers (*London Chronicle*, 26-29 July 1794; *The Times*, 28 July 1794) were enthusiastic.

Starred items were published separately (Hoskins, *Arnold*, 2:207-09; RISM A2204-06, also AA2203a). The printed libretto (London: G. Goulding, 1794) and song-words (London: T. Cadell & W. Davies, 1794) are in the Bodleian Library: Vet.A5e.1966(2); Vet.A5e.2009(1); Larpent Ms. 1033.

C20   RULE BRITANNIA!
Loyal sketch in 2 acts, music not extant
Libretto by James Roberts
First performed at the Haymarket Little Theatre, 18 August 1794

Larpent Ms. 1035 reveals that there were 10 vocal items, including some borrowings: an aria from Jean-Jacque Rousseau's *Le Devin du village* (1752) is sung by a French officer, and there is a song each by Ignaz Pleyel and Guiseppi Sarti. A chorus of sailors sing William Boyce's "Heart of oak" and the work ends with a "hornpipe dance of sailors" who also sing Thomas Arne's "Rule Britannia"; act 2 opens with the popular glee "Lord Mornington's waterfall." Arnold's own music includes a duet and a song each for Thomas and Annette, a chorus of gipsies, a sea-song, and a "Naval Overture." The text celebrates Howe's defeat of the French fleet at Ushant (1 June 1794). A copy of the printed libretto (London: Hookham & Carpenter, 1794) is in the British Library: 11777.c.85.

C21   BRITAIN'S GLORY (A TRIP TO PORTSMOUTH)
Musical entertainment in 1 act; music partially extant
Libretto by Robert Benson
First performed at the Haymarket Little Theatre, 20 August 1794

C21.1 Harriet's song

[London: Preston & Son, ca. 1794; RISM A2218]

C21.2 Susan's song

[London: Preston & Son, ca. 1794; RISM A2218]

C21.3 Captain Freeman's song

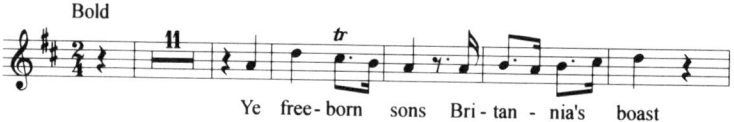

[London: Preston & Son, ca. 1794; RISM AA2218a]

This nautical work was written to commemorate a grand naval review held at Portsmouth in honor of George III's visit (28 June 1794). The extant songs are short and tuneful; according to the printed libretto (London: J. Barker, 1794; copy in the British Library: 643.f.2(1)), Arnold also composed a victory song celebrating Howe's successful campaign, a second song for Captain Freeman, and a finale. He appears to have borrowed James Hook's "Within a mile of Edinburgh" from *Harlequin and Faustus* (1793). Larpent Ms. 1036.

C / Afterpiece Operas with Spoken Dialogue

C22 **THE DEATH OF CAPTAIN FAULKNOR (BRITISH HEROISM)**
Opera in 1 act; music not extant
Libretto by William Pearce
First performed at Covent Garden, 6 May 1795

The text of this work is new but the music is partly William Shield's (lost) *Arrived at Portsmouth* (1794). This work commemorated the circumstances of Faulknor's daring frigate action and subsequent death at Guadeloupe (5 January 1795); Shield wrote funeral music and Arnold a new medley overture based on sea-songs. A copy of the printed libretto (London: Glindon & Co., 1795) is in the Bodleian Library: Vet.A5e.1966(9). The libretto reveals seven vocal numbers: three from *Arrived at Portsmouth* and four possibly by Arnold (including a medley of sea-songs opening with Thomas Arne's "Rule Britannia").

C23 **WHO PAYS THE RECKONING?**
Musical entertainment in 2 acts; music partially extant
Libretto by Samuel James Arnold
First performed at the Haymarket Little Theatre, 16 July 1795

C23.1   Emily's song (act 1)

[London: author, ca. 1795; RISM A2440-41]

C23.2   Mary's song (act ?)

[London: author, ca. 1795; RISM AA2436a]

The plot pivots on Emily, a virtuous village maid who defies the landlord-seducer and marries her soldier-sweetheart. This work was withdrawn after one performance but the music was liked. The *Morning Post*, 17 July 1795, mentions Arnold's "particularly good Martial Overture" with trumpet obbligato. The published song "A poor little gipsy" reappears in **C28** and **C30**. Larpent Ms. 1090; libretto reveals 8 vocal numbers, lost; also overture.

C24 **LOVE AND MONEY (THE FAIR CALEDONIAN)**
Musical farce in 1 act
Libretto by Robert Benson
First performed at the Haymarket Little Theatre, 29 August 1795

Printed vocal-keyboard score (London: Preston & Son, 2 September 1795, as op. 38; RISM A2284)

Singing characters: Jane (Elizabeth Kemble), Barbara (Elizabeth Leek); Peter (George Wathen), Jemmy (Miss Maria DeCamp)

C24.1   Scottish medley overture

C24.2   Opening song: Peter

Text incipits:

[Air: Peter]	Ere the lark's early carols
[Air: Jane]	When blest with my Jemmy ["Logie of Buchan"]
[Air: Jemmy]	See the stream (starred) so smoothly sliding ["Ar hyd y nos"]
[Duet: Jenny, Jemmy]	And shall I Jemmy's/Jenny's love retain
[Air: Jane]	Oh let me ne'er for fortune pipe
[Fnle: Jane, Jemmy, Barbara]	Then if our friends and patrons here

The highland peasants Jenny and Jemmy are unified despite the schemes of their unscrupulous landowner. Arnold's music mainly adopts the traits of Scottish folksong; Jane's airs first appear in the medley overture. "See the stream," set to the popular Welsh tune "All through the night," was published separately (Hoskins, *Arnold*, 2:224-25). A copy of the printed libretto (London: J. Wallis, [1798]) is in the Bodleian Library: Vet.45e.1382(7); Larpent Ms. 1092.

C25   **BANNIAN DAY**

Musical entertainment in 2 acts

Libretto by George Brewer

First performed at the Haymarket Little Theatre, 11 June 1796

Printed keyboard-vocal score (London: Longman & Broderip, 2 August 1796, as op. 39; RISM A2207)

Singing characters: Mrs. Goodwill (Elizabeth Leak), Polly (Maria Bland); Lieutenant Goodwill (? Trueman), Jack Hawser (George Wathen), Batch (John Fawcett), Bobby Notice (Richard Suett), Captain Macgallaher (John Johnstone)

C25.1   Overture

II. Rondo 2/4, D

C25.2   Opening song (act 1): Lieutenant Goodwill

C25.3   Opening song (act 2): Bobby Notice

Text incipits:
Act 1
   [Air: Lieut. Goodwill]   The man whose life is on the seas
   [Air: Mrs. Goodwill]   Hope still greets me
   [Air: Jack Hawser]   When on board the Hector
   [Air: Batch]   In my clubroom so great
   [Air: Polly]   It's Polly asks, can you deny?
   [Duet: Jack, Polly]   Come Polly let's be gay [William Reeve]

Act 2
   [Air: Bobby Notice]   At Symonds Inn I sip my tea
   [Air: Polly]   Tho' the lawyer comes to woo
   [Air: Capt. Macgallaher]   O 'tis mighty delightful
   [Air: Mrs. Goodwill]   O listen then and silent feel
   [Air: Jack Hawser]   When cruising off Brest
   [Fnle: Jack, Polly, Batch,   Now let joy and mirth go round
      Mrs. Goodwill, Bobby]

Against a naval setting Brewer explores the theme that virtue is always rewarded. Arnold's music is routine, but the finale movement of the overture and the closing ensemble bear interesting thematic resemblances to their counterparts in *Inkle and Yarico* (**B9**). The William Reeve item is possibly from William Shield's *Arrived at Portsmouth* (partially written by Reeve); see **C22**. This work had a short run (10 performances). There is a copy of the printed libretto (London: T. N. Longman, 1796) in the British Library: 11777.g.8; Larpent Ms. 1135.

C26   **THE SHIPWRECK**
Comic opera in 2 acts
Libretto by Samuel James Arnold
First performed at Drury Lane, 10 December 1796
Printed keyboard-vocal score (London: Longman & Broderip, 31 August 1796, as op. 40; RISM A2327)
Unchanged reissue (Longman, Clementi & Co., ca. 1798; RISM AA2327a)

A Thematic Index

Singing characters: Angelica (Elizabeth Leak), Sally Shamrock (Maria Bland), Fanny (Maria DeCamp); Dick (Master Thomas Webster), Shark (Thomas Caulfield), Goto (William Dowton), Selwyn (Charles Dignum), Stave (Richard Suett), Harry Hawser (John Bannister); chorus of wreckers

C26.1   Overture

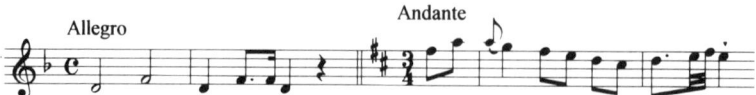

C26.2   Opening chorus (act 1): wreckers

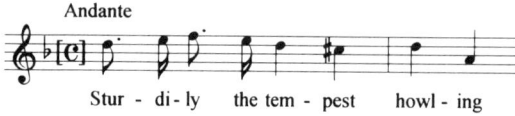

C26.3   Opening song (act 2): Angelica

Text incipits:

Act 1

[Chos: wreckers]		Sturdily the tempest howling [ATB; oboes and strings]
[Aria: Angelica]		Hope, thou balm and source of pleasure [oboe, bassoon, strings]
[Qt: Dick, Fanny, Shark, Goto]	+	Prythee ope your cottage door
[Aria: Selwyn]		O'er the ocean when sailors are roaming [strings]
[Air: Sally]	*	Come buy, who'll buy
[Duet: Sally, Stave]	*	In dear little Ireland
[Air: Dick]	*	On board the Valiant [clarinet, bassoon, strings]
[Fnle: Stave, Shark, Angelica, Harry]		Fetch the keys good Master Shark

Act 2

[Aria: Angelica]	*	With a heart light and gay [strings]
[Air: Stave]		Let women love water
[Air: Harry]		In the course of my life
[Air: Fanny]	*	When on the ocean
[Fnle: Dick, Selwyn, Angelica, Fanny, Harry, Stave, Sally]		Now the storms of life are over

The plot revolves around a coastal village that lives by wrecking, but the librettist's poor handling results in a melodramatic thriller, not a psychological drama between villains and victims. The *London Chronicle*, 10-13 December 1796, tells us that Arnold's music was well received ("Several songs were encored"). The orchestral resources required for performance are much more ample than those that Arnold typically employed. Cues for woodwind instruments punctuate the score, and some vocal items are printed with an extra staff to accommodate the string writing. Arnold's music contains vivid descriptions of the sea, especially in the storm overture and ensuing chorus. Dick's shanty-ish "On board the Valiant" is similar in style to "The Achilles tho' christen'd" from *Inkle and Yarico* (**B9**), and the chorus's depiction of sailors drowning recalls the sea-battle aria in *Gretna Green* (**C14**). The two arias for Angelica indicate what Arnold might have done had the text granted him more opportunity to develop character: in the heartbreak of the first, for example, rhetoric is balanced by sensuousness. The final vocal ensemble is based on the second movement of the overture.

Starred items were published separately (Hoskins, *Arnold*, 2:232-34; RISM A2329-37, also AA2329a-37a); a manuscript copy of "Prythee ope your cottage door" (crossed) is in the Royal College of Music: 2110(6), f. 19. Copies of the printed libretto (London: G. Cawthorn, 1797) and song-words (London: C. Lowndes, 1796) are in the British Library: 643.f.8(7); 11602.ff.31(12); Larpent Ms. 1146.

C27 THE HOVEL
Musical farce in 2 acts; music not extant
Librettist unknown
First performed at Drury Lane, 23 May 1797

Oulton, *Theatres*, 3:26, tells us that this "miserable trifle afforded no entertainment [and] . . . was neither repeated nor printed." Arnold is credited with the music (*The Times*, 23 May 1797). Larpent Ms. 1170; libretto reveals 9 vocal numbers, lost; also overture.

C28 THE IRISH LEGACY
Musical farce in 2 acts; music not extant
Libretto by Samuel James Arnold
First performed at the Haymarket Little Theatre, 26 June 1797

This work was stopped after two performances (*Morning Chronicle*, June 27: "it received strong marks of disapprobation"). The plot was devised to feature Jack Johnstone in his popular role as a blundering Irishman. According to the *Morning Chronicle* advertisement Arnold wrote an Irish medley overture. From Larpent Ms. 1176 we learn that Arnold included a self-borrowing ("A poor little gipsy" = **C23**; see also **C30**) and 12 other vocal numbers.

C29 THROW PHYSICK TO THE DOGS (JACK OF ALL TRADES)
Musical farce in 2 acts; music partially extant?
Libretto by Henry Lee
First performed at the Haymarket Little Theatre, 6 July 1798

A song "The bloom of inexperienced youth fades. The favourite air in Throw Physick to the Dogs" (no place or date of publication), is reported by RISM listing AA2418a to be in the State Library of Victoria, Melbourne, but it has not been successfully located.

This work ran only two nights. The *Morning Chronicle* of 7 July 1798 found the plot "absurd," and Oulton, *Theatres*, 3:18-19, calls attention to Arnold's uninspired music ("of very little assistance to the piece"). An edition of the song-words is in the Music Library, Yale University: M150.2/T523A82; Larpent Ms. 1221; song-words reveal 7 vocal numbers, possibly all lost; also overture. "The bloom of inexperienced youth" is sung by Augusta in act 2.

C30   THE REVIEW (WAGS OF WINDSOR)
Comic opera in 2 acts
Libretto by George Colman, the younger
First performed at the Haymarket Little Theatre, 1 September 1800
Printed keyboard-vocal score (London: John & Henry Caulfied, ca. 1801; RISM A2326)
Printed flute score (London: Preston, ca. 1808; copy: Mitchell Library, Glasgow: M9763)
Singing characters: Lucy (Rosemond Mountain), Phoebe (Maria DeCamp); Looney Mactwolter (John Johnstone), Charles (? Trueman), Caleb Quotem (John Fawcett); chorus of soldiers, villagers

C30.1 * Overture

II. Gavotto: moderato 4/4, d; Menuetto militaire 3/4, D

C30.2   Opening chorus (act 1): soldiers

C30.3   Opening song (act 2): Looney Mactwolter

C30.4   Two marches (act 2)

(solo fife)

Text incipits:
Act 1
    [Duet & Chos: soldiers]   When the lark in æther singing [unison chorus]
    [Air: Lucy]   * A poor little gipsy [= **C23**; oboe and strings]
    [Air: Phoebe]   A spruce little drummer
    [Glee: villagers]   Bacchus is a jolly boy [ATB]

Act 2
    [Air: Looney]   * Oh, whack, Cupid's a mannikin
    [Duet: Charles, Phoebe]   And will my love contented be
    [Air: Caleb]   I'm parish clerk and sexton here [William Shield (new)]
    [Fnle: villagers, soldiers]   Briskly, briskly beat the hollow drum [SATB]

Arnold's use of self-borrowings substantiates Colman's claim that this work was hurriedly written: the overture is that of Arnold's "military" pantomime *The Genius of Nonsense* (**E4**); the use of fifes, trumpets, and timpani heighten the military setting—at Windsor camp.

Starred items were published separately (Hoskins, *Arnold*, 2:250-52). A copy of the printed libretto (London: J. Cawthorn, 1808) is in the Bodleian Library: M.Adds. 109e.445, and the song words edition (London: Cadell & Davies, 1800) is in the Music Library, Yale University: lm.C711.800s; Larpent Ms. 1300.

C31   **THE VETERAN TAR (A CHIP OF THE OLD BLOCK)**
Comic opera in 2 acts
Libretto by Samuel James Arnold (after Charles-Antoine Pigault-Lebrun, *Le Petit Matelot*, 1796)
First performed at Drury Lane, 29 January 1801
Printed keyboard-vocal score (London: Thompson, 1801, as op. 50); copy in the British Library: H.104.a; other copies in the Pendlebury Library, Cambridge, Boston Public Library, and the Library of Congress.
Singing characters: Lisetta (Miss Stephens), Cicely (Rosemond Mountain); Henry (? Trueman), Farmer (Richard Suett), Philip (Vincent DeCamp), Tom Sturdy (John Bannister); chorus of villagers, sailors

C31.1 * Overture

Allegro

II. Andante 6/8, D; Rondo: [tempo unmarked] 2/4, D

A Thematic Index

C31.2   Opening duet (act 1): Lisetta, Cicely

C31.3   Opening chorus (act 2): sailors

Text incipits:
Act 1
  [Duet: Lisetta, Cicely]   Mild aurora softly smiling
  [Air: Cicely]   Yes I'll die an old maid
  [Trio: Cicely, Lisetta, Henry] + Hark, hark the village bells
  [Chos: villagers]   But see, unhappy omens [SSB?]
  [Air: Farmer]   When a man like myself
  [Air: Philip]   Against the rubs of life to guard
  [Air: Cicely]   When storms are sunk to rest
  [Air: Lisetta]   The sailor who ploughs the salt wave
  [Trio: Henry, Lisetta, Tom]   Come, shipwrecked sailor

Act 2
  [Chos: sailors]   Tom Clueline, Ben Bowling [ATB?]
  [Air: Philip]   The storm arose, the ship was lost
  [Duet: Tom, Philip]   Come ye little dog
  [Chos: villagers]   Let genuine pleasures here preside [SATB]
  [Duet: Philip, Cecily]   How shall I begin it well
  [Air: Cicely]   * Consult this joy-flush'd cheek
  [Air: Tom]   Odds life when a sailor
  [Fnle: villagers, sailors,   Swell aloud the conquering strain [SATB chorus]
    Philip, Tom]

The sailor-lover winning his rustic bride was a recurrent theme in English opera, and for this example Arnold provided the usual variety of short songs and simple ensembles. Both the overture and final chorus borrow popular patriotic songs; in the chorus, sailors sing Thomas Arne's "Rule Britannia" off-stage; this device had already been employed by Arnold in *Auld Robin Gray* (**C19**). The first chorus of villagers is similar in style to the storm chorus opening *The Shipwreck* (**C26**). In "Hark the village bells" Arnold imaginatively employs a miniature carillon to represent wedding bells; a manuscript copy of this item (+) can be located in the Royal College of Music: 2110 (SH 1948), f. 94. The overture and one song (*) were published separately (RISM AA2399a).

A copy of the printed libretto (London: J. Barker, 1801) is in the Bodleian Library: Vet.A5e.1947(3), and an edition of the song-words (London: C. Lowndes) is in the Music Library, Yale University: Ar64/801; Larpent Ms. 1314.

C32 THE SIXTY-THIRD LETTER (THE JOKE)
Comic opera in 2 acts
Libretto by Walley Chamberlain Oulton
First performed at the Haymarket Little Theatre, 18 July 1802
Printed keyboard-vocal score (London: Bland & Wellers, 10 August 1802, as op. 53); copies in Auckland Public Library: RBR782.6, and the Library of Congress: M3.A75(14)

Singing characters: Lydia (Rosemond Mountain), Patty (Sarah Harlowe), Miss Metaphor (Mary Ann Davenport); Casey (John Johnstone), Sidney (Vincent DeCamp), Dulcet (John Waddy), Sir Wilful (John Fawcett)

C32.1   Overture

II-III. Andante 4/4, d—Allegro 4/4, D

C32.2   Opening song (act 1): Lydia

C32.3   Opening song (act 2): Casey

Text incipits:
Act 1
[Air: Lydia]		Hence away with dismay
[Air: Lydia]	*	As t'other day in harmless chat [from Thomas Morton's *Beggar my Neighbour* (1802)]
[Air: Patty]	*	Harry came to me last week
[Air: Casey]	*	O the face of brave Captain Megan
[Qnt: Sidney, Dulcet, Patty, Metaphor, Wilful]		Fain I'd see my Lydia fair

Act 2
[Air: Casey]		When women are partners at cards ["Drops of brandy"]
[Air: Patty]		What tho' fine ladies
[Air: Dulcet]		Here are catches, songs and glees
[Air: Lydia]	*	In my eyes dear Edward read
[Fnle: Lydia, Sidney, Patty, Dulcet, Casey]		Let us all forgive the past

A THEMATIC INDEX

Arnold's score was hurriedly written and, according to Oulton, *Theatres*, 3:34-35, was not sufficiently attentive to the libretto's needs ("[the] music was of no assistance"). *The Times* reviewer of 20 July 1802 described the music as "dull and insipid." Almost all the songs are in rudimentary ballad style; one for Dulcet includes snippets from patriotic airs. The title refers to an "elopement" letter from an epistolary novel, which is taken as true.

Starred items were published separately (Hoskins, *Arnold*, 2:260-61; RISM AA2342a-d). A copy of the printed libretto (London: J. Barker & Son, 1802) is in the Bodleian Library: Vet.A5e.1969(3); Larpent Ms. 1353.

D / Pasticcios and Other Operas with Contributions by Arnold

D1 **DAPHNE AND AMINTOR**
Pasticcio "comic opera"; Prologue and 1 act
Libretto by Isaac Bickerstaffe (after Susanna-Maria Cibber's translation of *L'Oracle* by Georges-François Saint-Fox)
First performed at Drury Lane, 8 October 1765
Printed keyboard-vocal score (London: Robert Bremner, 8 November 1765; RISM BII:149)
Printed flute score (London: Robert Bremner, ca. 1765; RISM BII:149)
Music drawn from: [Samuel Arnold?], Gioacchino Cocchi, Baldassare Galuppi, Pierre Monsigny, Niccolò Piccini, ? Shalon, Mattia Vento

Contribution possibly by Arnold:

D1.1   Duet: Daphne, Amintor

This work is attributed to Arnold in two sources: RISM AA2239b and R. Alec Harman, *A Catalogue of the Printed Music and Books on Music in the Durham Cathedral Library* (London: Oxford University Press, 1968), 92. It has been associated with Arnold on the basis of his collaboration with Bickerstaffe in *The Maid of the Mill* (**B1**); the extent of Arnold's contribution, if any, is uncertain. A copy of the printed libretto (London: J. Newbery and others, 1765) is in the Bodleian Library: 17405e.149(2).

D2 **THE SUMMER'S TALE**
Pasticcio "musical comedy" in 3 acts
Libretto by Richard Cumberland
First performed at Covent Garden, 6 December 1765

D / Pasticcios and Other Operas with Contributions by Arnold

Printed keyboard-vocal score (London: J. Walsh, 3 vols., 19 December 1765, 6 and 29 January 1766; RISM BII:378)
Printed flute score (London: J. Walsh, 1765; RISM BII:378)
Music drawn from: Carl Abel, Thomas Arne, Samuel Arnold, Johann Christian Bach, Joseph Baildon, Ferdinando Bertoni, William Boyce, John Lampe, Giovanni Lampugnani, Niccolò Piccini, Passuale Potenza, Ferdinand Richter, Count of Saint Germain, John Stanley, Joseph Vernon

Contributions by Arnold:

D2.1 Song (act 1): Sir Anthony Withers

D2.2 Song (act 1): Bellafont

D2.3 Song (act 2): Bellafont

D2.4 Chorus of peasants (act 2): SATB

D2.5 Song (act 3): Bellafont

D2.6 Song (act 3): Amelia

Memoirs of Richard Cumberland, Written by Himself (London, 1806-07), 186-87, indicates that this work was written hurriedly and that the score was a collaboration ("Abel furnished the overture, [Johann Christian] Bach, Doctor Arne and Arnold supplied some original compositions"). The pasticcio was intended to eclipse the success of *The Maid of the Mill* (**B1**); both share a rustic setting but Cumberland's libretto, unlike Bickerstaffe's, did not allow many opportunities to create comedy of character in musical terms. There was a short run of ten performances. This work was later altered to make the two-act "musical entertainment" *Amelia* (Drury Lane, 14 December 1771; music not extant). According to the libretto of *Amelia* (London: T. Beckett, 1771), all but Amelia's air of Arnold's contributions were deleted and six new songs were composed by Charles Dibdin. A copy of the printed libretto of *The Summer's Tale* (London: J. Dodsley and others, 1765) is in the Bodleian Library: M.Adds.IIIe.39(8); Larpent Ms. 249.

D3   **TOM JONES**
Pasticcio "comic opera" in 3 acts
Libretto by Joseph Reed (after Henry Fielding's novel, 1749)
First performed at Covent Garden, 14 January 1769
Printed keyboard-vocal score (London: Welcker, 14 January 1769; RISM BII:390)
Music drawn from Carl Abel, Michael Arne, Thomas Arne, Samuel Arnold, Johann Christian Bach, William Boyce, Arcangelo Corelli, ? Cox, Baldassare Galuppi, ? Granom, George Frideric Handel, Johann Hasse, Henry Holcombe, Pierre Van Maldere, Giovanni Pergolesi, Niccolò Piccini

Contributions by Arnold:

D3.1 * Opening song (act 1): Tom

D3.2   Song (act 1): Mrs. Honour

D3.3   Song (act 1): Sophia

D3.4 Closing duet (act 1): Tom, Sophia

D3.5 Song (act 2): Sophia

D3.6 Song (act 3): Sophia

D3.7 Duet (act 3): Nightingale, Nancy

The Gazetteer of 16 January 1769 claims that Arnold and Edward Toms compiled the music, but it may have been that Thomas Arne was involved since Arnold and Arne together contributed about a quarter of the score. Fielding's bawdiness and buffoonery are absent from Reed's libretto, which is based on an expurgated version the French author Alexandre Poinsinet had written for François-André Philidor's Paris opera of 1765. **D3.1** (starred) was published separately in full score (two oboes, two horns, and strings; RISM A2437). A copy of the libretto (London: Beckett, and De Hondt and others, 1769) is in the Bodleian Library: Vet.A4e.1950(7); Larpent Ms. 290.

D4 **AMINTAS**
Pasticcio "English opera" in 3 acts
Libretto by Ferdinando Tenducci (an adaptation of Richard Rolt's *The Royal Shepherd*, 1764, based on Pietro Metastasio)
First performed at Covent Garden, 15 December 1769
Printed keyboard-vocal score, 2 vols. (London: Welcker, 1770; copy in Harvard University Library: Rare M. 1503/E58t; vol. 1 in British Library, Royal College of Music, Library of Congress; vol. 2 in King's College, Rowe Music Library; vol. 3 not extant)

A Thematic Index

Music drawn from Samuel Arnold, Thomas Carter, Tommaso Giordani, Pietro Guglielmi, François Philidor, Jean-Philippe Rameau, George Rush

Contributions by Arnold:

D4.1 Song (act 1): Amintas

D4.2 Song (act 1): Alexander

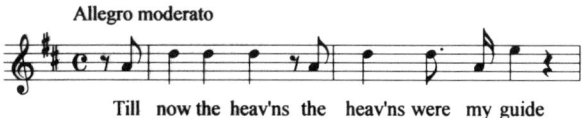

D4.3 Song (act 1): Alexander

D4.4 Song (act 2): Alexander

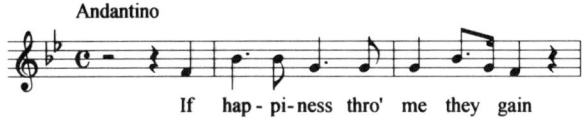

D4.5 Song (act 2): Eliza

The music is mainly taken from George Rush's setting of *The Royal Shepherd*, but items by Arnold and Carter are new. The story is about two pairs of lovers who, under the patronage of Alexander the Great, represent the theme of love versus state. A copy of the libretto (London: T. Lowndes, 1769) is in the Bodleian Library: Vet.A5e.1951(6).

D5 **TRUE BLUE (THE PRESS GANG)**
"Musical interlude" in 1 act
Words and music by Henry Carey
Performed "with alterations" at Covent Garden, 12 November 1770

From comments in *The Town and Country Magazine* 22 (November 1770): 593, Carey's afterpiece was revived because of the imperialistic message—press gangs contribute to victory. Carey's *Nancy: or, The Parting Lovers* (1739), later titled *True Blue: or, The Press Gang* (1755), was first performed at Covent Garden on 1 December 1739; the song-sheets were published together in April 1740 (see Fiske, *Theatre Music*, 156). The music for the 1770 revival is credited to Arnold in *Monthly Mirror* 10 (March 1803): 227, but nothing of it survives. If Arnold was involved, it is possible he collaborated with George Colman, the elder.

D6 **THE SERAGLIO**
Comic opera in 2 acts
Libretto by Charles Dibdin with Edward Thompson; music by Charles Dibdin
First performed at Covent Garden, 14 November 1776
Printed keyboard-vocal score (London: John Johnston, 1776; RISM D2673)

Contributions by Arnold:

D6.1   Song (act 1): Venture

D6.2   Song (act 2): Lydia

D6.3   Finale (act 2): Abdullah, Frederick, Reef, Polly

This "Turkish" opera was completed by Arnold when Dibdin was exiled in France to avoid imprisonment for debt and sticky emotional entanglements (see Fiske, *Theatre Music*, 378-80). **D6.1** is a parody of Mungo's syllabic chatter-song in Dibdin's *The Padlock* (1768). It appears from an autograph score in the British Library (Add. Ms. 30955, ff. 69r-73v) that Arnold composed an earlier version of this song and fully orchestrated it (for oboes, bassoons, and strings) before forsaking it. The earlier version, in minor mode, is arguably the most appropriate choice; the vocal line begins:

D6.4

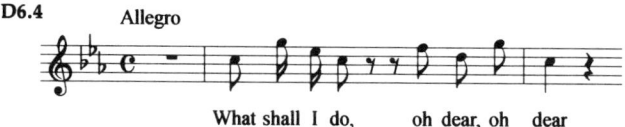

A Thematic Index

A copy of the libretto (London: T. Evans, 1776) is in the Bodleian Library: Malone B.39(6); Larpent Ms. 418.

D7 **POLLY**

Ballad opera in 3 acts, written in 1729 as a sequel to *The Beggar's Opera* of 1728
Libretto written by John Gay, altered by George Colman, the elder, for the first performance
Musical arrangements attributed to Johann Christoph Pepusch, revised with new music by Arnold for the first performance; Arnold's orchestral score is in the Harvard University Library: Houghton fMS Mus 97
First performed at the Haymarket Little Theatre, 19 June 1777

Contributions by Arnold:

D7.1   Overture (medley of tunes from *The Beggar's Opera*, 1728; strings, oboes, bassoon, horns, harpsichord)

= "Cotillon" (air 22, *The Beggar's Opera*)

D7.2.   Song (act 1): Polly (strings, flutes, bassoon, harpsichord)

D7.3   Song (act 1): Polly (strings, oboes, bassoon, horns, harpsichord)

D7.4   Song (act 1): Trapes/Mrs. Ducat? (strings, bassoon, harpsichord)

D7.5   Song (act 1): Mrs. Ducat (strings, oboes, bassoon, harpsichord)

D7.6a   Pirates Dance (entr'acte; strings, harpsichord)

D7.6b   Hornpipe (violins 1)

D7.6c   Andante (violins 1)

D7.6d   Hornpipe (violins 1)

D7.6e   Allegro (violins 1)

D7.7   Dead March (act 2): Polly falls asleep (strings, oboes, bassoon, horns, harpsichord)

D7.8   Duet (act 2): Morano, Jenny (strings, oboes, bassoon, horns, harpsichord)

D7.9   Song (act 2): Vanderbluff (strings, oboes, bassoon, harpsichord)

A Thematic Index

D7.10 Song (act 2): Jenny (strings, oboes, bassoon, harpsichord)

In love and life the pre-sent use

D7.11 Duet (act 2): Jenny, Polly (strings, oboes, bassoon, horns, harpsichord)

Jenny: We ne-ver blame the for-ward swain

D7.12 Song (act 2): Cawwawkee (strings, oboes, bassoon, harpsichord)

The bo-dy of the brave may be ta-ken

D7.13 Song (act 3): Ducat (strings, flute, oboes, bassoon, harpsichord)

What man can on vir-tue or cou-rage re-pose

D7.14 Song (act 2): Polly (strings, harpsichord)

The sports-men keep hawks and their quar-ry they gain

D7.15 Song (act 3): Ducat (strings, oboes, bassoon, harpsichord)

I hate the fool-ish elf

D7.16 Duet (act 3): Polly, Cawwawkee (strings, flutes, bassoon, horns, harpsichord)

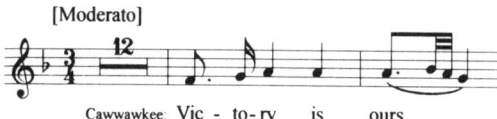
Cawwawkee: Vic-to-ry is ours

D7.17 Song (act 3): Morano (strings, oboes, bassoon, horns, harpsichord)

D7.18 Song (act 3): Polly (strings, flutes, bassoon, harpsichord)

D7.19a Dance of Indians (opening act 3 finale; strings, oboes, horns, bassoon, harpsichord)

D7.19b

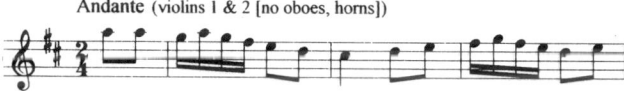

D7.19c

D7.19d

D7.19e

A THEMATIC INDEX

Concordance to text incipits:
Act 1

[Air: Trapes]	The manners of the great affect ["The disappointed widow" in 1729 lib. and Ms. score, not 1777 lib., probably not performed]
[Air: Ducat]	He that weds a beauty ["Noel Hills" in 1729, 1777 libs., Ms. score]
[Air: Trapes]	Observe the statesman's ways ["Polwart on the green," tune set to "Love now is nought" in 1729 lib., 1777 songwords adapted from "In pimps and politicians" (1729)]
[Air: Polly]	She who hath felt a real pain [newly-composed by Arnold, words in 1729 lib. set to "Sortez des vos retraites"]
[Air: Polly]	Farewell all hope of bliss! [newly-composed by Arnold, words in 1729, 1777 (erroneously) libs. set to "Waly, waly"]
[Air: Trapes/Mrs. Ducat?]	Despair is all folly ["O Jenny come tye me" in 1729, 1777 libs., Ms. score also includes a variant setting, "Air for Mrs Love" (Catherine Love who played Mrs. Ducat), newly-composed by Arnold]
[Air: Mrs. Ducat]	I will have my manners ["Red House" in 1729 lib. and Ms. score, not 1777 lib., probably not performed]
[Air: Ducat]	When billows are breaking ["Old Orpheus tickl'd" in 1729, 1777 libs., Ms. score]
[Duet: Ducat, Mrs. Ducat]	When a woman jealous grows ["Christ-church bells" in 1729, 1777 libs., Ms. score]
[Air: Damaris]	When kings by their huffing ["Cheshire-rounds" in 1729, 1777 libs., Ms. score]
[Air: Polly]	The crow or daw thro' all the year ["Johnny Farr," words in 1729 lib. set to "The bush aboon Traquair"]
Duet: Polly, Ducat]	How can you be so teazing? ["Bury fair" in 1729, 1777 libs., Ms. score]
[Air: Ducat]	Fond maids like courtiers ["The Coterie," in Ms. score but not 1777 lib., probably not performed, words in 1729 lib. set to "Bobbing Joan"]
[Duet: Ducat, Mrs. Ducat]	Brave boys prepare ["March in *Scipio*, i.e., Handel, *Scipione* (1726); set as a trio in 1729 lib.]
[Air: Damaris]	Better to doubt ["Jig-it-o'foot" in 1729, 1777 libs., Ms. score]
[Air: Mrs. Ducat]	Abroad after misses most husbands will roam ["Trumpet minuet," newly-composed by Arnold, replaces 1729 setting]
[Air: Polly]	The stag when chas'd ["Tweedside," ends act 1 in 1777 lib. and Ms. score, act 2, scene 13 in 1729 lib.]

Act 2

[Air: Polly]	Why did you spare him ["La villanella" in 1729, 1777 libs., Ms score]
[Air: Laguerre]	Patriots at first aloud declare ["La cavalliere" in 1777 lib. and Ms. score, not 1729 lib.]
[Air: Culverin]	Cheer up my lads ["Minuet" in 1729, 1777 libs., Ms. score]
[Duet: Morano, Jenny]	Shall I not be bold [newly-composed by Arnold, words in 1729 lib. set to "Sawney was tall and of noble race"]
[Air: Jenny]	When gold is in hand ["Peggy's mill" in 1729, 1777 libs., Ms. score]
[Air: Vanderbluff]	Woman's like the flatt'ring ocean [newly-composed by Arnold, words in 1729 lib. set to "Ton humeur est Catharine"]
[Air: Morano]	Tho' different passions rage by turns ["The boatman," words in 1729 lib. set to "Since the world's turn'd upside down"]
[Air: Polly]	The world is always jarring ["Hunt the squirrel" in 1729, 1777 libs., Ms. score]
[Air: Jenny]	In love and life the present use [newly-composed by Arnold, words in 1729 lib. set to "Young Damon once the lovliest swain"]
[Duet: Jenny, Polly]	We never blame the forward swain [newly-composed by Arnold, words in 1729 lib. set to "Catharine Ogye"]

[Air: Jenny]	My heart is by love forsaken ["Roger a Coverly" in 1729 lib. and Ms. score, not 1777 lib., probably not performed]
[Air: Cawwawkee]	The body of the brave may be taken [newly-composed by Arnold, words in 1729 lib. set to "Cappe de bonne esperance"]
[Air: Morano]	Honour calls me from my arms ["Excuse me" in 1729, 1777 libs., Ms. score]
[Air: Jenny]	Honour plays a bubble's part ["Reuben" in 1729, 1777 libs., Ms. score]
[Air: Morano]	We the sword of valour drawing ["The Marlborough," act 2 finale in 1777 lib., in 1729 lib., sung by Cawwawkee in act 3]

Act 3

[Air: Ducat]	What man can virtue or courage repose [probably newly-composed by Arnold, words not in 1777 lib., probably not performed, words in 1729 lib. set to "There was an old man and he liv'd"]
[Duet: Cawwawkee, Polly]	Virtue's treasure ["T'amo tanto" in 1729 (act 2), 1777 libs., Ms. score; replaced by "The sportsmen"]
[Air: Polly]	The sportsmen keep hawks [two versions, one "Lochaber," the other newly-composed by Arnold, in Ms. score, not 1777 lib., Arnold's version in late rehearsals, words in 1729 lib. set to "Down in a meadow"]
[Air: Cawwawkee]	Love with beauty is flying ["O saw ye my father," words in 1729 lib. set to "Iris la plus charmante"]
[Air: Morano]	When the tyger roams ["Prince Eugene's march" in 1729, 1777 libs., Ms. score]
[Air: Ducat]	I hate the foolish elf [probably newly-composed by Arnold, words not in 1777 lib., probably not performed, song-words modelled on "I hate those coward tribes" in 1729 lib.]
[Air: Cawwawkee]	The turtle thus upon the spray ["Kate of Aberdeen" (1777 lib.), words in 1729 lib. set to "Thro' the wood laddie," both versions in Ms. score]
[Duet: Polly, Cawwawkee]	Victory is ours [newly-composed by Arnold, words not in 1777 lib., probably not performed, words in 1729 lib. set to "Clasp'd in my dear Melinda's arms"]
[Air: Morano]	The soldiers, who by trade must dare [newly-composed by Arnold, words in 1729 lib. set to "Parson upon Dorothy"]
[Air: Polly]	Can words express ["Young Jockey was the blythest lad," words not in 1777 lib., probably not performed, words in 1729 lib. set to "Blithe Jockey young and gay"]
[Air: Polly]	My heart forbodes he's dead [Thomas Arne, "Shall man," *The Death of Abel* (1744), words in 1729 lib. set to "One evening as I lay"]
[Chos: Indians]	Justice long forbearing ["The temple" in 1729, 1777 libs., Ms. score]

Houghton fMS Mus 97 is the score of the 1777 and later Haymarket Little Theatre productions; the copyist is unknown but revisions in Arnold's and in other later hands are included; violin 2 parts dated 1782. The Houghton score contains various arrangements (keeping less than half of Pepusch's printed music), including the only extant version of Arne's "Shall man" from *The Death of Abel* and newly-composed music by Arnold, including a medley overture of airs from *The Beggar's Opera* (the 1729 libretto and songs includes no overture), 15 songs (some of which were cut), a "dead march," and 10 instrumental dances. The medley overture is introduced by air 22, "Cotillon"; this one-movement work employs full scoring, in contrast to the entr'acte "Dance of Pirates" for strings only and the finale "Dance of Indians," which contains a lot of unison scoring. Twelve original parts rebound separately or in sets of 2 into 7 volumes:

1. (harpsichord = short score) 62f. (110 pp.)
2. (violin 2, 2x) 37f. (59 pp.) and 33f. (58 pp.)
3. (violin 1, 2x) 40f. (64 pp.) and 33f. (56 pp.)
4. (bass [violoncello, bassoon], 2x) 33f. (59 pp.) and 31f. (51 pp.)
5. (horn 1, horn 2) 12f. (22 pp.) and 13f. (20 pp.)
6. (viola) 28f. (51 pp.)
7. (oboe/flute 1, oboe/flute 2) 19f. (34 pp.) and 14f. (27 pp.)
   24.5x30cm (vol. 1); 31x24cm (vols. 2-7).

This set, together with the 1729 libretto, annotated as acting copy in 1777 (Harvard TS 2526.200), and the 1777 libretto (London: T. Evans), annotated as prompt copy in 1782 (Harvard TS 2526.201) and Larpent Ms. 431, constitutes the complete performance material for George Colman the elder's first production of *Polly* (1777) and the revised performances of 1782.

In *Polly* the leading characters of the *The Beggar's Opera*, Polly Peacham (soprano) and Macheath (tenor, disguised as a Negro, Morano), are transported to the West Indies where the action takes place. Gay's story of coffee planters, pirates, and Indians continues to explore the issues of sexual and economic exploitation central to *The Beggar's Opera*, but moves in the direction of sentimentality and a more straight-forward kind of morality culminating in the execution of Morano and the union of faithful Polly to the virtuous Indian prince Cawwawkee. Though the libretto contains little that was politically sensitive, *Polly* was banned during rehearsal in December 1728 by the Lord Chamberlain (perhaps through the influence of Sir Robert Walpole). The first performances of Colman's cut version were moderately successful: the singing was liked, except for Hester Colles in the title role, who possessed a good tone but sang off-key (*Morning Post*, 20 June 1777).

For a discussion of the original tunes, see A. E. H. Swaen, "The Airs and Tunes of John Gay's *Polly*," *Anglia* 60 (1936), 402-22, and Claude M. Simpson, *The British Broadside Ballad and Its Music* (New Brunswick: Rutgers University Press, 1966). For a discussion of Arnold's music, see Hoskins, *Arnold*, 1:161-64, 299-306. My edition of Arnold's overture is published by Artaria Editions, no. AE088 (Wellington, New Zealand, 1997), and my edition of the complete opera for Artaria Editions is forthcoming.

D8 **THE SHEEP-SHEARING**
Pastoral in 3 acts
Libretto by George Colman, the elder (altered version of David Garrick's adaptation of William Shakespeare's *The Winter's Tale*)
Music by Thomas Arne; Arnold's additional songs not extant
First performed at the Haymarket Little Theatre, 18 July 1777

Garrick in *The Sheep-Shearing*, Covent Garden, 25 March 1754, revived as *Florizel and Perdita*, 22 December 1760, had drastically cut Shakespeare's play from five to three acts and concentrated interest on the later rustic scenes, transferring many of Shakespeare's best passages and also adding new lines for Autolycus the pedlar and some explanatory material; Garrick's libretto was published, but not Arne's music. Colman's text inserted two new songs for Florizel in act 2; these were set by Arnold. This work had only one performance during the season; according to the *Morning Chronicle*, 19 July 1777, Charles Du-Bellamy as Florizel "sang well," but Colman's abridgement was judged "slender and unsubstantial." A copy of Colman's libretto (London: G. Kearsly, 1777) is in the Bodleian Library: Vet.A5e.1957(1).

D9 **A FAIRY TALE**
Pastoral in 2 acts
Libretto by George Colman, the elder (altered from David Garrick's adaptation of William Shakespeare's *A Midsummer Night's Dream*)
Music by Michael Arne; Arnold's additional music not extant
First performed in a Shakespeare double-bill (see **D8**, above) at the Haymarket Little Theatre, 18 July 1777

The libretto of *A Fairy Tale* was a slightly shortened version of the adaptation that Colman had made of Garrick's *A Midsummer Night's Dream* for Drury Lane in 1763; a copy of *A Fairy Tale* (London: J. and R. Tonson, 1763) is in the Bodleian Library: Vet.A5e.1952(7). Michael Arne's four songs from the 1763 score were incorporated in the Haymarket Little Theatre production, together with new music by Michael Arne, Samuel Arnold, Charles Dibdin, and James Hook. The new music, including Arnold's contribution—a finale for act 2—is not extant. See Gooch and Thatcher, *Shakespeare Music*, 2:972-73; also Fiske, *Theatre Music*, 317. George Winchester Stone, Jr., in "*A Midsummer Night's Dream* in the Hands of Garrick and Colman," *PMLA* 327 (June 1939): 467-82, and Alfred Loewenberg in "*A Midsummer Night's Dream* Music in 1763," *Theatre Notebook: A Quarterly of Notes and Research* 1 (April 1946): 23-26, provide detailed accounts of both productions. Stone's article is meticulously detailed, but tends to minimize Colman's contribution to the return to Shakespeare's text.

D10 **POOR VULCAN**
Burletta in 2 acts
Libretto and music by Charles Dibdin
First performed at Covent Garden, 4 February 1778
Printed keyboard-vocal score (London: J. Johnston and W. Randall, 5 February 1778; RISM D2580)

Contributions by Arnold:

D10.1 Duet (act 1): Joe

D10.2 Song (act 2): Joe, Maud

This work was completed by Arnold when Charles Dibdin was in exile (see **D6**). **D10.1** is based on the Irish folksong "Allen Aroon"; in **D10.2** the combination of voice and solo cello is designed to heighten a sense of tenderness. The text parodies "Classical deities": Vulcan and Venus have permission to live in England and run a pub there. A copy of the libretto (London: G. Kearsly and W. Nicoll, 1778) is in the Bodleian Library: Vet.A5e.1957(5); Larpent Ms. 443.

D11 THOMAS AND SALLY (THE SAILOR'S RETURN)

According to a playbill issued by the Haymarket Little Theatre on 24 February 1794 (see British Library, *Playbills* 113, no. 138), Arnold provided "a new finale" to Thomas Arne's afterpiece opera *Thomas and Sally* (1760); no copy is known.

D12 VIRGINIA
Comic opera in 3 acts
Libretto by Dorothea Plowden (after Mary Pix, *The Innocent Mistress*, 1697; also
    Aphra Behn, *The Widow Ranter*, 1690)
Music by Dorothea Plowden, arranged by Samuel Arnold
First performed at Drury Lane, 30 October 1800
Printed keyboard-vocal score (London: Clementi, Banger, Hyde, Collard & Davis,
    1800, as [Plowden's] op. 1; RISM P4960)
Singing characters: Alphonso (Michael Kelly), Beauclerc (John Bannister), Bodkin
    (Richard Suett), Sea-officer (Thomas Sedgwick); Benowee (Arabella Menage),
    Blanche (Miss Stevens), Gertrude (Anne Biggs), Jennet (Rosemond Mountain),
    Matilda (Anna Crouch); chorus of sailors, soldiers, workmen, natives

D12.1   Overture

D12.2   Opening chorus (act 1): soldiers, sailors, workmen, natives

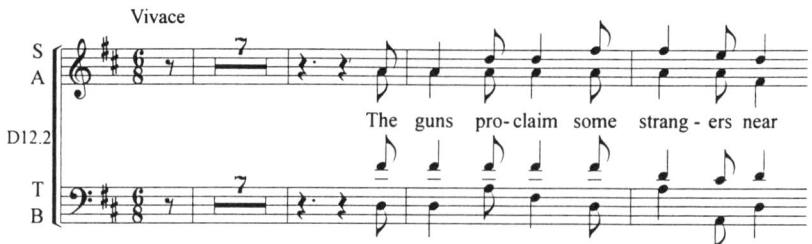

D12.3 March "On the landing of the Soldiers" (act 1)

D12.4 Duet (act 2): Jennet, Blanche

D12.5 Air (act 3): Gertrude

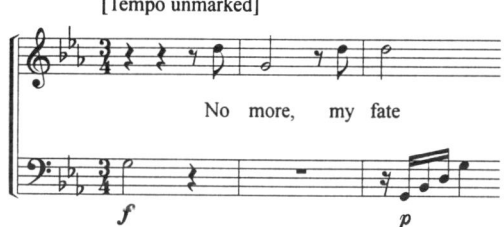

Text incipits:

Act 1

[Chos: soldiers, sailors, workmen, natives]	The guns proclaim some strangers near [SATB]
[Qt: Jennet, Matilda, Blanche, Bodkin]	Great news! What? Pray good Bobby tell us
[Qt: Bodkin, Matilda, Blanche, Jennet]	Who'd believe that did not hear
[Air & chos: Alphonso, sailors, soldiers, workmen, natives]	Nor wealth, nor birth, nor skill, nor pow'r [SATB]
[Air: Bodkin]	Oh dear, oh dear
[Air: Benowee]	Save me, save me, white man save me
[Fnle: sailors, soldiers, workmen, natives]	Grateful Manteo is thy name [SATB]

Act 2

[Duet: Jennet, Blanche]	Love's a tender timid passion
[Air: Jennet]	Excuse me, my dear, but I think you conceited
[Air: Gertrude]	In this dilemma, what can I say Sir

A THEMATIC INDEX

[Air: Matilda]	How sweetly glide the minutes o'er
[Air: Blanche]	A lively young maiden of blooming eighteen
[Aria: Alphonso]	To bid adieu to her I love
[Fnle: chorus of Europeans]	Hymen's delights they wish to prove [SATB]

Act 3
[Air: Gertrude]	No more my fate is cast, fond hope adieu
[Air: Jennet]	Young Moggy and Peggy had sweethearts to meet
[Duet: Alphonso, Matilda]	Ah, sweet Matilda stay
[Air: Sea-officer]	Fair Kitty gave to all delight
[Duet: Beauclerc, Bodkin]	Here is a day, a day of wonders
[Fnle: Gertrude, Benowee, Alphonso, Matilda; chorus of sailors, soldiers, workmen, natives]	Fell sorrow's gone by, dull gloom is dispering [SATB]

The play, a love-intrigue set in the newly founded colony of Virginia among hostile natives, ran only one night. Critics disliked Plowden's script, but the *Morning Chronicle* of 31 October 1800 found the music "very pleasing." In the preface to the libretto, Plowden credits the opera's failures to a series of disasters which led to the first night; she observes that Arnold, her former composition teacher, "harmonised" the "melodies" and was horrified at the music being so under-rehearsed. A copy of the libretto (London: J. Barker, 1800) is in the Bodleian Library: Malone.B.45(3); Larpent Ms. 1303.

E / Pantomimes

E1 **HARLEQUIN DR. FAUSTUS**
Pantomime in 1 act
Libretto by Henry Woodward (after Lewis Theobald's *The Necromancer: or, Harlequin Dr. Faustus*, 1723)
First performed at Covent Garden, 18 November 1766
Printed keyboard-vocal score (London: Welcker, 1766; RISM A2255)
Singing characters: Helen of Troy (Elizabeth Baker); Miller (Charles Dubellamy), ? (Charles Dibdin)

E1.1   Opening song: Helen of Troy

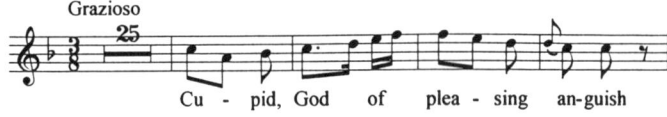

1. Song: Helen of Troy, "Cupid, God of pleasing anguish"
2. Song: Miller, "Haste my lads your lasses bring"
3. Allegro 6/8, G ("Country dance")

4. Allegro 4/4, G ("Furies")
5. Pomposo, 4/4, B♭ ("The miller going to the doctor")
6. Vivace 3/8, G ("Doctor's study")
7. Song: ?, "You'll wonder sage doctor"
8. Andante 4/4, d ("The miller crying")
9. Allegro moderato 4/4, D ("Eagle scene")
10. Un poco andante 3/4, G ("The rising of the bowers")
11. Andante 3/4, g ("The statues")
12. Allegro moderato 4/4, g ("Hurry")
13. Vivace 4/4, G [untitled]
14. Allegro 3/4, D ("Alderman's house")
15. [Tempo unmarked] 4/4, G ("Hall pursuit")
16. Minuetto vivace 3/4, C ("Ladies dressing room")
17. Minuetto vivace 3/4, D ("2^d part of the Ladies dressing room")
18. Con larco 2/4, G ("The clock")
19. [Tempo unmarked] 6/8, F ("The screen")
20. [Tempo unmarked] 2/4, G ("Bed chamber")
21. [Tempo unmarked] 6/8, C ("Mill tune")
22. Presto 9/8, G ("Pursuit)
23. Larghetto 4/4, c ("Harlequin going home")
24. [Tempo unmarked] 4/4, E♭ ("Harlequin's last scene")
25. [Tempo unmarked] 2/4, G ("Country scene")
26. Song: Miller ("Our cares are all vanish'd")
27. [Tempo unmarked] 2/4, D ("Country dance")
28. [Tempo unmarked] 3/4, G ("Dusty Miller") [occurs in Medley Overture no. 6 by Peter Prelleur? and was probably written for John Galliard's original *Harlequin Dr. Faustus* (1723)]
29. [Tempo unmarked] 2/4, D [*Pas de deux*: "Mr Fisher, Miss Wilford"]
30. Andante 4/4, G [*Pas de deux*: "Mr Fisher, Sig^{ra} Manefiere"]
31. Allegro 6/8, G ("Giga")
32. [Tempo unmarked] 2/4, D ("Contradanza")

Arnold's new music for *Harlequin Dr. Faustus* was published complete in a single volume resembling a keyboard-vocal score. Before this, pantomime music, if published at all, appeared in a haphazard way, with a few songs in sheet form and a selection of comic tunes on their own. Arnold's score includes strophic songs for Dibdin and Dubellamy and one in binary form for Elizabeth Baker; in the comic tunes much of the music is effectively designed to match specific moments in the action, and several numbers are printed on three staves to accommodate the string writing. Henry Woodward, a first-class comic actor and Harlequin, played the title role. According to the *British Chronicle*, 19-21 November 1766, the performance was a great success. Larpent Ms. 259 is song-words only.

E2   **THE RAPE OF PROSERPINE**
Pantomime in 1 act; possibly John Galliard's score with new music by Samuel Arnold; new music not extant
Libretto an altered version, possibly by Ferdinando Tenducci ? of Lewis Theobald's *The Rape of Proserpine* (1727)
First performed with new material at Covent Garden, 4 November 1769

The *Monthly Mirror* 10 (March 1803): 227, credits Arnold with writing new music for the Theobald-Galliard pantomime, but the extent of Arnold's contribution, if any, is uncertain. According to the *Public Advertiser*, 6 November 1769, the production was well received and included spectacular scenographic effects; the reviewer observed that "The serious Part of the Pantomime . . . was entirely new." For an account of the original pantomime see Fiske, *Theatre Music*, 81-84.

E3 **MOTHER SHIPTON**
Pantomime in 1 act
Libretto by George Colman, the elder
First performed at Covent Garden, 26 December 1770
Printed keyboard-vocal score (London: Welcker, 1771; RISM A2291)
Singing characters: Mother Shipton (Frederick Reinhold), Shepherd (Charles Dubellamy)

E3.1   Overture

E3.2   Opening instrumental number ("First scene")

E3.3   Opening song: Shepherd

Overture: Allegro 3/4, D

1. Allegro 2/4, G ("First scene")
2. Andante 4/4, c [untitled]
3. Allegro 6/8, D ("The wood")
4. Andante 6/4, g ("Mother Shipton's house")
5. Allegro 6/8, A ("Fairies' dance")
6. Menuetto 3/8, B♭ ("Chamber") +
7. Allegro 2/4, G [untitled]
8. Allegro 2/4, D ("Tower scene")
9. Pomposo 4/4, B♭ ("Thames")
10. Allegro 4/4, D ("Hurry")
11. [Tempo unmarked] 6/4, F ("Baker's shop")
12. [Tempo unmarked] 2/2, G ("Cornhill")
13. Allegro 4/4, D ("Apple orchard")

14. Andante 2/4, E♭ [untitled]
15. Allegro moderato 2/4, D [untitled]
16. Vivace 4/4, B♭ ("Hay-stack")
17. Allegro 6/8, D ("Country dance")
18. Menuetto 3/8, D [untitled]
19. Allegro 6/4, B♭ ("Grotto") +
20. Allegro 2/4, A [untitled]
21. Moderato 6/8, C ("Cooper's tune")
22. Jigg 6/8, F ("A view of the coal pit")
23. Menuetto 3/8, D ("Mother Shipton's house")
24. [Tempo unmarked] 2/2, g ("Inside of a coal pit")
25. March 2/4, D [untitled]
26. Andante 4/4, D ("Dance, Mr Fisher and Mrs Manefiere")
27. [Tempo unmarked] 4/4, B♭ [*Pas de deux*: "M^r and Mrs Hamoir"]
28. Allegro 6/8, D ("Country dance")
29. Song: Shepherd, "To heal the wound a bee had made" [violins 1-2 and lower strings]* +
30. Song: Mother Shipton, "'Tis true I'm a fright"
31. Song: Mother Shipton, "Tho' the pit my son has swallow'd"

This pantomime, based on a famous Yorkshire sorceress, achieved lasting popularity; startling scenographic effects included "A view of the world rising out of nowhere." In the score the comic tunes are printed at the beginning and all the songs at the end. Of the songs, Mother Shipton's "Tho' the pit" is the most individual: the vocal line paints the word "thunder" with eighth-note scales and the section "flash ye lightnings, rumble thunder" anticipates the second song in *Harlequin Teague* (E5). The opening instrumental number, "First scene," is retitled "Farmyard" in William Shield's pantomime *Harlequin's Museum: or, Mother Shipton Triumphant* (1792).

The starred item was published separately (RISM AA2291a; also Hoskins, *Arnold*, 2:269). Manuscript copies (crossed) of numbers 6, 19, and 29 are in Glasgow University Library: Bi.22z.29, pp. 60-63. No libretto is extant; song-words (London: n.p., 1770).

E4   **THE GENIUS OF NONSENSE**
Pantomime in 1 act
Libretto by George Colman, the elder
First performed at the Haymarket Little Theatre, 2 September 1780
Printed keyboard-vocal score (London: for the author by Harrison & Co., 5 November 1784, as op. 27; RISM A2250)
Printed flute score (London: Harrison & Co., 1 December 1784; RISM A2251)
Singing characters: Ballad singer (Miss Lyon), Columbine (Catherine Morris), Genius of Nonsense (Miss Hooke); Dame Turton (John Edwin), Gammar Gurton (Charles Bannister), Goody Burton (Charles Wood), Harlequin (John Bannister), Head of the Marine Society (Master John Edwin), Medical patients (Charles Bannister, William Brett, William Davies, John Edwin), Officer in the Camp (Charles Wood)

E4.1   Overture [= C30]

   II. Gavotto: moderato 4/4, d
   III. Minuetto Militaire 3/4, D

E4.2   Opening song: Genius of Nonsense

Overture: Allegro 4/4, D; Gavotto: Moderato 4/4, d; Minuetto militaire 3/4, D

1. Song: Genius of Nonsense, "Oh follow, then, where Nonsense points the way" [anon., "The dressing room," *Harlequin Ranger* (1752)]*
2. Song: Harlequin, "Yes thou goddess fair and free" [Charles Burney, "The animating Harlequin," *Queen Mab* (1750)]
3. Duet: Watchman, Harlequin, "Past six o'clock!" [Charles Burney, "The watchman," *Queen Mab* (1750)]
4. Andante 6/8, A ("Street scene") ["Pantomime tune" (?)]
5. Minuetto 3/4, G ("Chamber scene")
     Trio (1) 3/4, C
     Minuetto da capo
     Trio (2) 3/4, C
     Minuetto da capo
6. Presto 4/4, D ("Pursuit")
7. Catch: Dame Turton, Goody Burton, Gammar Gurton, "Neighbours, neighbours, once in a way" [Henry Purcell, "Soldier take off thy wine," catch *a* 4 (ca. 1682-90)]
     Recit.: Gammar Gurton, "Tho' the warm and youthful dame"
     Catch da capo
     Air: Dame Turton, "Youth will not return"
     Catch da capo
8. Catch: Dame Turton, Goody Burton, Gammar Gurton, "Look, neighbours, look" [Dr. Henry Harrington, "Look, neighbours, look" catch *a* 3 (ca. 1780)]
9. Pomposo 4/4, c ("Scene, Westminster Abbey")
10. Andante 6/4, E♭ ("The viewing of the tombs")
11. Slow 4/4, g ("Harlequin disconsolate")
12. [Tempo unmarked] 2/2, D ("Becket's Yard")
13. Air: Columbine, "Oh where e're you chance to rove" [George Rush, "Vows of love should never end," *The Royal Shepherd* (1764)]
14. Moderato 6/8, B♭ ("The road to Chatham")
15. Moderato 6/8, A ("Flower Garden")
16. March 4/4, D ("View of Chatham, when the Marine Society enters")
17. Song: Head Boy of the Marine Society, "Come, cheer up my lads" [William Boyce, "Heart of Oak," *Harlequin Invasion* (1759)]
18. [Tempo unmarked] 4/4, D ("Hornpipe")

19. Moderato 6/8, G ("Street, with the quack doctor's two men")
20. Song: Ballad singer, "All folks labour with disease" ["Nancy Dawson" (1760)]
21. Medical catch: [Four patients], "Can you cure master doctor, a very bad hand?"
22. Allegretto 6/8, B♭ [untitled]
23. [Tempo unmarked] 9/8, a ("Going to the Camp") ["O my kitten"]
    [Tempo unmarked] 2/4, c ["Going to the Camp"]
24. Song: Genius of Nonsense, "'Tis thus with a wife" [oboes, bassoons, strings]
25. Song: Officer, "Hark where the trumpet now calls you to arms" ["The Belle-Île march," (ca. 1760)]
26. [Tempo unmarked] 6/8, G ("Dance in the camp")
27. Anthem: [Marine Society], "God save great George our king"

A "speaking" pantomime, *The Genius of Nonsense* was subtitled "An Original, Whimsical, Operatical, Pantomimical, Farcical, Electrical, Naval and Military Extravaganza." Dr. James Graham's miracle cures—the "Temple of Health" and "Celestial Bed"—are satirized in the action, and although Colman's libretto was never published many descriptions appeared in the newspapers (for example, the *Morning Chronicle* of 4 September 1780). For Colman's authorship, see Richard Peake, *Memoirs of the Colman Family* (London: Bentley, 1841), 2:54. Larpent Ms. 532 (transcribed in Burnim, *Colman 1*, 5).

In the first movement of the overture the use of trumpets, trombones, and kettledrums emphasizes the military atmosphere (there are scenes laid in the camp at St. James's Park), as does the opening theme of the finale, first played by two trumpets and later repeated by bassoons and the penetrating C clarinets. Of the vocal music, the "medical catch," in which patients' requests for a cure is set against the doctor's prescription for treatment by electricity, is much the most interesting. The instrumental piece "Dance in the camp" was used previously by Arnold in *Summer Amusement* (1779), and originally to begin the second movement of his seventh lesson for harpsichord, op. 10, book 1.

The starred item was published ("with the permission of Dr. Arnold") in the August issue of the *European Magazine*, 1782 (RISM A2252). A copy of the printed song-words (London: T. Cadell, 1780) is in the Bodleian Library: Vet.A5e.1949(2); Larpent Ms. 532. According to the song-words there was a contribution by Johann Christian Bach for Ann Cargill as the Goddess of Health, but the music has not survived; the vocal score also excluded Arnold's song for John Bannister in the "Supper" scene, which included various farmyard imitations.

E5   **HARLEQUIN TEAGUE (THE GIANT'S CAUSEWAY)**
Pantomime in 1 act
Libretto by John O'Keeffe and George Colman, the elder
First performed at the Haymarket Little Theatre, 17 August 1782
Printed keyboard-vocal score (London: S. A. & P. Thompson, 1782, as op. 19; RISM A2256)
Singing characters: Columbine (Catherine Morris); Genius of Ireland (William Brett), Giant of the Causeway (Master W?, Brett), Landlord of the "Horns" at Highgate (Richard Wilson), Lieutenant of the press-gang (John Edwin), Man with two heads (Charles Bannister)

A Thematic Index

E5.1   Overture

II. Allegro 6/8, D ["Irish Medley"]

E5.2   Opening song: Genius of Ireland

Ten thou-sand times   a-round the globe

Overture: Allegro 4/4, D; Allegro 6/8, D

1. Air: Genius of Ireland, "Ten thousand times around the globe"
   Recit.: Genius of Ireland, "Erin and Albion, sister isles"
   Air: Genius of Ireland, "Flash lightnings, roll thunder"
2. Song: Giant of the Causeway, "The Irish you shall find" [Charles Dibdin, Vauxhall Watch ("My name's Ted Blarney"), *The Touchstone* (1779)]
3. [Tempo unmarked] 6/8, D ("Scene Highgate") ["Pompey and Caesar were both of them horned"]
4. Song: Landlord, "Silence, take notice, you're my son" [Irish bagpipe tune very popular as "Out of my sight" in John O'Keeffe and William Shield, *The Poor Soldier* (1782)]*
5. Allegro 6/8, D ("Scene the street")
6. Vivace 2/4, C ("Scene the chamber")
7. Presto 2/4, F ("When the coach breaks down")
8. [Tempo unmarked] 2/4, F/f ("Scene the road with the finger post") [oboes in minor section]
9. Vivace 6/8, B♭ ("Scene the street") [Carolan's "Planxty O'Connor"; see Fiske, *Theatre Music*, 612]
10. Vivace 6/4, B♭ ("The parrots scene")
11. Song: Columbine, "His presence gives birth" [flute and strings]*
12. [Tempo unmarked] 3/4, C ("The Press gang")
13. Song: Genius of Ireland, "Twas I learn't a pretty song in France" ("Fal de ral tit")*
14. Vivace 2/4, E♭ ("When Drury Lane theater changes to a puff shop")
15. [Tempo unmarked] 3/4, D ("When they cross to the E.O. table")
16. [Tempo unmarked] 6/8, D ("Scene E.O. table")
17. [Tempo unmarked] 4/4, a ("Hurry when the constables come")
18. [Tempo unmarked] 6/8, a ("Scene the street")
19. [Tempo unmarked] 2/2, B♭ ("Scene floor cloth warehouse")
20. Vivace 6/8, F/d ("When the scene changes into a garden")
21. [Tempo unmarked] 2/4, a ("The street with umbrellas")
22. Andante 3/4, d ("The saloon")
23. [Tempo unmarked] 6/8, A/a ("Chamber scene at night")
24. Amoroso 9/8, D ("When Pierrot goes to sleep")
25. Vivace 4/4, D ("When Pierrot is tied in a blanket")
26. [Tempo unmarked] 6/8, C ("Scene street")
27. Glee: Anchor Smiths, "Smiths are good fellows" [John Cobb's catch *a* 4 "Smiths are good fellows" (1642)]*
28. [Tempo unmarked] 4/4, g ("Scene the Anchor Smith's shop")
29. [Tempo unmarked] 2/4, c ("Scene Ranelagh") [clarinets, bassoons, and horns]
30. Song: Man with two heads, "Ere the sun lifts his head" [flutes, horns, strings]

The second movement of the overture sets the scene with an "Irish Medley," beginning with "Jacky Bull" (which is in fact English), played first by solo bassoon and cello. The first scene is laid out in a rather unusual manner. The orchestra begins with an *allegro* flourish, to which presumably the Genius of Ireland entered, and then there follows a suitably dignified air and recitative wherein the Genius tells how Cormac, the leader of the giants, conspired to dethrone him but was defeated and imprisoned in the Causeway. Suddenly there is a storm and plentiful rushing figures for strings to depict thunder and lightning. Next, "the Magician, by a stroke of his wand calls forward the Giant of the Causeway and tumbles down several of the largest pillars in which he is confined" (*Public Advertiser*, 20 August 1782). As the man with two heads, Bannister was given a "solo duet" wherein the different characters of sportsman and dandy are wittily portrayed, their differences being used to motivate the contrasts of rhythm and instrumentation.

According to John O'Keeffe, George Colman, the elder, sought his advice about the libretto (O'Keeffe, *Recollections*, 2:46-47); the libretto was not published but a report in the *London Chronicle*, 17-20 August 1782, gives us a good idea of its content. A copy of the printed song-words (London: T. Cadell, 1782) is in the Bodleian Library: Douce S.143 (14); Larpent Ms. 600 (transcribed in Burnim, *Colman 1*, 5). Starred items were published separately (Hoskins, *Arnold*, 2:279-80; RISM A2257-58).

E6 **HERE AND THERE AND EVERYWHERE**
Pantomime in 1 act; music not extant
Libretto by Carlo Antonio Delpini
First performed at the Haymarket Little Theatre, 31 August 1785

According to Larpent Ms. 706, the music included a bird-catcher's song ("Hark, hark 'tis the linnet") and another "written & to be sung by Mr. Delpini." The *Morning Chronicle*, 1 September 1785, gives a lengthy synopsis of the action; we learn William Meadows's bird-catcher's song "received . . . the most thundering applause."

E7 **THE GNOME (HARLEQUIN UNDERGROUND)**
Pantomime in 2? acts; music partially extant
Libretto by Ralph Wewitzer and Kiza? Invill
First performed at the Haymarket Little Theatre, 5 August 1788

E7.1   Sailor's song, "Smiling Nan" [= F2]

(London: Harrison & Co., ca. 1788; RISM A2253)

The only detailed report is from the *London Chronicle* for 5-7 August 1781; Charles Bannister sang the sailor's song. The song words for "What should sailors do on shore?," "Make from for a jolly stone-eater," and "The ladies cannot but approve" were printed in the *Public Advertiser*, 6 August 1788. Libretto not extant.

E8 **HARLEQUIN PEASANT (A PANTOMIME REHEARSED)**
Pantomime in 1 act; music not extant
Librettist unknown
First performed at the Haymarket Little Theatre, 26 December 1793

According to the printed song-words (London: T. Cadell, 1793), a copy of which is in Yale University Library, Maria DeCamp as Columbine sang "Quand le bien aimé reviendra" from Nicolas-Marie Dalayrac's *Nina* (1786); there were five other vocal items. The reviewer for the *London Chronicle*, 26-28 December 1793, liked DeCamp's "two or three very beautiful" songs and noted that Charles Dignum "sung a sweet air or two" in the role of Harlequin. Larpent Ms. 1001.

E9 **OBI (THREE FINGER'D JACK)**
Pantomimical-drama in 2 acts
Libretto by John Fawcett (after the story of Jack Mansong in Benjamin Moseley's *A Treatise on Sugar*, 1799, revised 1800)
First performed at the Haymarket Little Theatre, 2 July 1800
Printed keyboard-vocal score (London: John Longman, Clementi & Co., 13 November 1800, as op. 48; RISM A2315)
Singing characters: Planter (Thomas Caulfield), Quashee (John Emery), Overseer (Thomas Trueman); Rosa (Maria DeCamp), Sam's wife (Anne Gaudry), Quashee's wife (Rosemond Mountain)

E9.1   Overture

[Thomas Linley, "Dance of Savages" from *Robinson Crusoe*, 1781]

E9.2   Negro duet opening act 1

The white man comes and brings his gold

E9.3   Instrumental number opening act 2

Overture: Pomposo e stacato 3/4, d—Allegro non presto, D

Act 1
1. Duo: Quashee's wife, Sam's wife, "The white man comes"
   Chos: Negroes, "Good Massa we find" [SATB]
   Trio: [Negroes], "We love Massa"
   Chos: Negroes, "Good Massa we find" [SATB]
   Air: Overseer, "Black Ladies and Gentlemen"
   Chos: Negroes, "Sing tingering" [SATB]
2. Andantino 6/8, a ("Overseer examines the work")
3. Allegro 2/4, C ("Tuckey the Negro servant enters")
4. Moderato 3/4, G [untitled]
5. Recit: Planter, Overseer, "Yes, yes, he has landed"
6. Vivace 2/4, C ("Tuckey introduces Captn Orford")
7. March 4/4, B♭ ("Negro March")
8. Andante 2/4, G ("Rosa the Planter's daughter enters") [flute, strings]
9. Moderato 2/4, E ("The Captn and Tuckey start")
10. Allegro 2/4, C [untitled]
11. Vivace 2/4, a ("Sports of Negro's [sic]")
12. Agitato 2/4, A / A little slower, a [bassoon, strings] / Tempo 1°, A / Slower, a [bassoon, strings] / Andante 2/4, A [Mozart, Andante of String Quartet in D, K. 575]
13. Air & Chos: Overseer, Negroes, "Swear by the silver crescent of the night" [ATB chorus]
14. Vivace 3/8, F / Slower [untitled]
15. Moderato, Gavotto 4/4, F [untitled; oboes, horns, strings]
16. Allegretto ma non troppo 6/8, d [untitled; Mozart, D-minor String Quartet finale, K. 421/417b]
17. Bold, Allegro 4/4, B♭ [untitled]
18. Andante 2/4, E♭ [untitled; solo oboe, strings]
19. Sprightly and bold 6/8, C ("Dance of Negros")
20. Vivace 2/4, G [untitled]
21. Slow 2/4, C [untitled]
22. Vivace 6/8, a [untitled]
23. Allegro moderato 6/8, F [untitled]
24. Andante 2/4, E♭ [untitled]
25. Vivace 6/8-2/4, B♭ / Slow 2/4, g / Vivace 6/8, B♭ ("Noise by Jack is heard")
26. Andante 4/4, G [untitled]
27. Vivace 2/4, D / Resoluto [untitled]
28. Quick March 4/4, G [untitled]
29. Andante 4/4, G / Allegro / Tempo 1° [untitled]
30. Bold 4/4, B♭ [untitled]
31. Duo: Quashee, Quashee's wife, "Quashee he load his gun"
32. Duo for two fifes 2/4, G
33. Bold 3/4, G ("Quashee is christen'd")
34. Finale: Quashee's wife, Sam's wife, chorus of Negroes, "We Negro men and women"

Act 2
35. Vivace 2/4, D [untitled]
36. A little slower and bold 2/4, D [untitled]

37. Un poco piu e moderato 2/4, G [untitled]
38. Air: Quashee's wife, "My cruel love to danger go"
39. Andante 2/4, C-c [Haydn, Andante of G-major Symphony no. 94 ("Surprise")]
40. Allegro moderato 4/4, E♭ ("The Storm")
41. Andante 6/8, E♭ [Haydn, Andante of Piano Trio in D, Hob. XV:24]
42. Vivace 3/8, G [untitled]
43. Moderato 2/4, B♭ [untitled; solo clarinet & bassoon, strings]
44. Andante 4/4, G / Faster ("Inside of Jack's cave"; "Jack sings")
45. Air: Rosa, "A Lady in fair Seville city"
46. Andante 3/8, D / Resoluto 2/4 / A little faster 3/8 [untitled]
47. Allegro 4/4, B♭ ("Jack awakes")
48. Slow 2/4, D [untitled]
49. Vivace 6/8, D [untitled; strings "con sordini"]
50. Slow 2/4, F / resoluto 2/4, d / Allegro 3/8, g / Slow 3/8, d [untitled]
51. Amoroso e staccato 2/4, F [untitled]
52. Allegro moderato 4/4, D [untitled]
53. Slow 6/8, a [untitled; solo flute, strings]
54. Air: Quashee's wife, "You never hear of Mandingo king" [John Davy (newly-composed)]*
55. Vivace 2/4, A [untitled]
56. Pastorale 6/8, F [untitled]
57. Moderato and bold 4/4, D [untitled]
58. Allegro 2/4, G [untitled]
59. [Tempo unmarked] 4/4, D ("Combat between Jack and Quashee")
60. [Tempo unmarked] 3/4, b ("When Jack dies")
61. Allegro 4/4, E♭ [untitled]
62. March 2/4, d [untitled]
63. March 2/4, d [untitled]
64. Finale: Quashee's wife, Sam's wife, Overseer, unison chorus, "Wander now to and fro" [František Kočzwara, "The Battle of Prague"]

Obi: or, Three Finger'd Jack is the first of three innovative pantomimes by Arnold in which an action-packed story is mimed by actors to continuous orchestral music, with occasional vocal numbers interspersed. *Obi* is based on the Jamaican story of Jack Mansong, a Negro outlaw driven by the horror of slavery to revolt. The pantomime explores the conflict between Jack and the plantation community while adding the love of Rosa and Captain Orford, the roles of the Negro wives and Obi-woman, and the saga of imprisonment and rescue. The triumph of Christianity, stressed in Fawcett's version, ensures a kind of happy issue—the death of Jack, driven beyond endurance by hostile, heathen forces, will restore order.

One of the most interesting aspects of Arnold's score is the variety of musical structure, ranging from a simple two strain duo (act 1, no. 31) to big closed forms, like the one for Rosa's entrance (act 1, no. 8); from a short four-bar ground (act 2, no. 56) to the use of a motto-like theme that permeates act 2, no. 57, then is sounded in no. 59 to signal the battle between Jack and Quashee. Especially striking in *Obi* is Arnold's inventive dovetailing of sections, as at the beginning of act 1. These 146 measures of continuous music, including ten changes of time and seven changes of performing forces, produce a purely musical "grand opening" to the pantomimical drama. Similar dove-tailings occur in other parts of the score, but there the shape of the music is cut to fit the stage action. In the borrowed music Arnold's invariable method is to employ an element of parody, and he makes use of the music in a variety of ways: in the "Surprise" movement of Haydn and the opening 24 measures of Mozart's Allegretto, K. 421, the music remains unchanged, but in other cases it is freely adapted.

Important as a starting point for any study of *Obi* are the source materials relating to the pantomime, including Fawcett's manuscript libretto (Larpent Ms. 1297), the printed wordbook, issued in London 1801 by Thomas Woodfall, which contains song-texts and a "Prospectus of the Action" (copy in the British Library: C.108.bbb.65), and the printed piano-vocal score, which includes stage directions helpful in correlating action to music. In addition, reviews containing actual performance details—notably Thomas Dutton's in the *Dramatic Censor* 3 (London, 1801): 16-29—and the Harrison/Orme depiction of Jack's cave (Harvard Theater Collection) are interesting for the insight they provide about the staging of the production.

For a full discussion of this work, including a table of the narrative and placement of musical numbers, see the critical introduction by Robert Hoskins with Eileen Southern to the facsimile reproduction of the keyboard-vocal score, *Music for London Entertainment* (series D, vol. 4, 1996, xi-xxix). Starred items were published separately (Hoskins, *Arnold*, 2:290-92). See also Charles J. Rzepka, "Thomas De Quincey's 'Three-Fingered Jack': The West Indian Origins of the 'Dark Interpreter'," *European Romantic Review* 8 (1997): 117-38.

E10   **THE CORSAIR (THE ITALIAN NUPTIALS)**
Ballet-pantomime in 2 acts
Libretto by Charles Farley (after Ann Radcliffe's gothic fictions and Matthew Lewis, *The Castle Spectre*, 1797)
First performed at the Haymarket Little Theatre, 29 July 1801
Printed keyboard-vocal score (London: Wigley & Bishop, 8 August 1801, as op. 51; RISM AA2239a)
Singing characters: Gramberio (Thomas Caulfield), Granchio (? Trueman); chorus of fishermen, villagers

E10.1   Overture

E10.2   Instrumental number opening act 1

E10.3   Fishermen's duet opening act 2: Gamberio, Granchio

A THEMATIC INDEX

Act 1
1. Pastorale 6/8, G-V^7/D — "The Rising of the Sun"
   "Fiorita enters and decorates her Bower"
2. March 4/4, D — "Rugoso teaches his Children the art of War"
   Slower 6/8, G — "Fiorita returns to the Bower"
   March 4/4, D — "Rugoso teaches his Children again"
3. Sprightly but not too quick 3/4, A — "Gagliardo enters"
   Slower 4/4, D-V^7/G
4. March: Sprightly 4/4, G — "Procession and Dance"*
5. Chos: villagers, — "Welcome Love, welcome Joy" [SATB]
   [repeat no. 4] — "for Procession going off"
6. Andante 4/4, c-V^7/C — "When the Vessel appears and crosses the Stage"
7. Slow 4/4, C — "Corsair appears" [includes "bells solo"]
   [repeat no. 4] — "Procession Returns to go into the House"
8. Not too quick 3/4, E♭ — "Gagliardo and Fiorita alone"
9. [Tempo unmarked] 3/4, c — "Corsair enters Enraged"
10. Moderato 6/8, E♭ — "The Corsair Enters"
    Rather faster 4/4, E♭ — "Corsairs Enter"
11. Brisk and lively 2/4, G — "Rugoso Gagliardo and Villagers Discover'd"
12. [Tempo unmarked] 2/4, C — "Dance by Miss Menage"*
    [repeat no. 11]
13. Moderato 2/4, B♭-g — "Gagliardo Fiorita Rugoso and Julio" [solo violin & orchestra]
    E♭-V^7/B♭ — "The Air darkens"
    B♭ — ["Da Capo"]
14. [Tempo unmarked] 3/4, B♭ — "Eruption of Mount Vesuvius"
15. Andante 4/4, d — "Tomar Enters"
    Presto 4/4, d — "Corsair Enters. Gets in at window"
16. Sprightly 6/8, G — "Inside the Cottage"
17. Bold and sprightly 3/4, C — "Rugoso and Gagliardo"
18. Slow 4/4, g — "Gallery. / Tomar searches for Fiorita / Fiorita enters and goes to her devotions / Tomar surprizes her / Gagliardo enters / The Fight / Whistle / Door broke open / Tomar bears her away / Gagliardo follows / They stop him / he jumps out of window"
19. Moderato 2/2, B♭ — "Inside of cottage. Corsairs force away Rugoso and Children"
20. Bold 2/4, G — "Scene the Sea, Corsair Enters with Fiorita / forces her into vessel / Whistle is heard / Tomar shoots Rugoso
    Slower g
    Tempo primo g
    Slower
    Tempo primo — Children &c carry Rugoso off"
21. Andante 6/8, F — "Cave. Quieto in Chains"
22. Moderato 4/4, D — "The Sea. Vessels sailing. Moon light"
23. Bold 4/4, B♭ — "Grate Opens. Corsairs Enter"
24. Allegro 4/4, g/B♭ — "Tomar Enters with Fiorita / Corsairs Enter with Gagliardo / Chain Fiorita and Gagliardo"
    [B♭ = 23]
25. Andante 4/4, E♭-c — "Corsairs go off" [solos for flutes & horns]
26. Moderato 2/2, F — "Sun Rises"
    Slower d — "Quieto descends
    Allegro g-D — Quieto shoots Guard
    Moderato D — unchains Gagliardo and Fiorita unlocks Grate / Kills other Guard / Tomar and Corsairs Enter / Vessel seen passing with Quieto &c."

Act 2
27. Duet: fishermen,   "Let others complain"
28. Gay 6/8, D   "Gagliardo Fiorita and Quieto Enter from Boat / Fishermen come out of the hut"
29. Minuetto 3/4, E♭   "Julio in search of the Lovers" [includes solo violin melody]
30. Vivace 6/8, E♭   "Finds the Cross / Gagliardo Enters and meets Julio
     Andante c   Julio relates the death of Rugoso
     A Tempo E♭   They go into the Hut"
31. Moderato 6/8, d   "Vessel Passes.
           A   Tomar and Corsairs Enter"
           d
32. Polacca 3/4, D   "The Party Enters from Hut to repast"
           d
           D
33. Hurry 4/4, A   "Pistol heard"
34. Resoluto 2/2, D   "Tomar Enters disguised as a Fisherman
           A   Discovers himself"
           D
35. Allegro moderato 4/4, g   "a Whistle is heard and Corsairs Enter
         E♭-V^7/g   They fight
         g   Tomar throws Julio from the Rock
         E♭-V^7/g   Fiorita fires Pistol
         g   she flies
36. [Tempo unmarked] 4/4, D   "The Fight between Gagliardo Quieto and four Corsairs / Corsairs fly"
37. Andante 3/4, g   "Gagliardo wounded / Julio groans Gagliardo brings him on wounded / tells him the capture of Fiorita"
38. Hurry 4/4, g-V   "Exit"
39. Hurry 4/4, a   "Forest. Fiorita flying from Tomar"
40. Andante 6/8, a   "A Corsair enters see Fiorita and calls on his companion"
41. Strong and firm 4/4, A   "Corsairs draw lots for Fiorita"
42. With energy 3/4, D   "Quieto rescues Fiorita"
43. Slow 4/4, d   "Tomar enters
     Amoroso D-A-D   Quieto enters with Fiorita"
44. Bold 4/4, D   "Tomar and Quieto fight for Fiorita"
45. Fishermen and chorus of fishermen   "Lead on Gagliardo" [Chos: SATB]
46. Andante 4/4, g-V   "Inside of Tomar's Castle"
47. March 4/4, G   "Corsairs Enter
        D-G   followed by Tomar and Fiorita"
48. Sempre piano 4/4, E   "Tomar offers Presents"
49. Resoluto 4/4, A   "Tomar struggles with Fiorita
     Slower d   ariel Hand seizes Tomar / Hand disappears [score includes gong strokes]
     [Resoluto?] A   Spectre appears"
50. Andante 4/4, D   "Spectre points to his wound and beckons Tomar to Staircase
     Bold d   ascends staircase
     D   Spectre admonishes Tomar [flutes & horns]
     V^7-D   Tomar fires
     Allegro D   Building falls"
51. Andante 6/4, D   "Spectre ascends" [flutes & violins]
52. Allegro 4/4, g-V   "Shout. Gagliardo &c. Enter and destroy Tomar and Corsairs"
53. Andante 6/8, g   "Tomar dies"

A Thematic Index

Charles Farley's script replicates the gothic plots of murder, usurpation, the maiden endangered with abduction, the masculine tyrant in his castle lair. The lovers move through many adventures of romantic horror, including an eruption of Mount Vesuvius, but the ghost of the murdered Rugoso provides the only element of the supernatural. In the music, chromatic unease keeps the "psychology of terror" present to our minds all the way through; the score contains skillful employment of romantic coloring in the orchestra, including muted horns, gongs, and bells.

Starred items were published separately (Hoskins, *Arnold*, 2:297-98; RISM A2239). An edition of the printed wordbook containing song-texts and a "Prospectus of the Action" (London: T. Woodfall, [1801]) is in Yale University Library (the "Prospectus of the Action" is reprinted in the *Morning Chronicle* review, 31 July 1801); Larpent Ms. 1330.

E11   **FAIRIES' REVELS (LOVE IN THE HIGHLANDS)**
Burletta and ballet in 1 act
Libretto by John Fawcett (after "The Ring," a dramatic poem by Thomas Little [i.e., Thomas Moore], 1801)
First performed at the Haymarket Little Theatre, 14 August 1802
Printed keyboard-vocal score (London: J. & H. Caulfield; ? August 1802; RISM A2244)
Singing characters: Fairy Queen (Miss Tyrer), Film (Miss Howells); chorus of fairies

E11.1   Overture

II. [Tempo unmarked] 4/4, G ["Blue bells of Scotland"—"Reel"]

E11.2   Opening air and chorus: Queen, fairies

= E11.1 now in G

E11.3   First of the concluding "Dances by the various Characters"

Overture: [Slow] 4/4, d—Light and airy 6/8, D; [tempo unmarked] 4/4, G ["Blue bells of Scotland"—"Reel"]

Scene 1

1. Song & chos: Queen, fairies, "Come to the east"   [= overture 6/8, D, now in G]

Scene 2

2. [Tempo unmarked] 3/4, G   "Enter Donald deploring the loss of Isabel" ["Tweedside"]
3. [Tempo unmarked] 2/4, G   "Enter Isabel unobserved / she comes behind Donald puts a band over his eyes, and playing with him some time discovers herself / he promises to fly with her from her Father's power" ["Saw ye my father"]
4. Con furia 2/2, B♭   "They are surpriz'd by her Father / he takes her away {Donald left in despair is met by Film disguised as a Witch}"
5. Song: Film, "What causes my Donald this pain"   [bassoon solo, strings]

Scene 3

6. Resoluto 4/4, c   "Enter Old Man with Isabel / He threatens her / She cries
   Quicker E♭   the old man calls Jane and Peggy
   Slower c   he tells them of Isabel's conduct
   Quicker E♭   they affect to be shock'd
   Quicker c   The old man drives Isabel in to the House
   E♭   a signal is heard
   Slower E♭-c   Jane answers it / Malcolm appears on the wall
   Quicker E♭   Peggy is sent to watch the Old Man"
7. Moderato 4/4, E♭   *Pas de deux*: Malcolm, Jane (Master and Miss Geroux)
8. Andante 4/4, D   "The Old Man enters / enquires who has been there / they assume ignorance / he appears satisfied
   Allegro A   but returning stumbles over Malcolm's bonnet
   Andante D   another signal is heard, which the Old Man answers
   Allegro D   the lovers return over the wall, and are detected
   Andante D   The Old Man asks them what they can do to deserve their Mistresses"
9. [Tempo unmarked] 4/4, G   "Malcolm answers he can dance"
10. Moderato 6/8, E♭   *Dance*: Malcolm
11. Vivace 2/4, C   "The Old Man is pleased with Malcolm's Dance, asks Donald, who declines"
12. [= "Blue bells of Scotland movement in the overture]   "Isabel Dances for him"
13. [Tempo unmarked] 4/4, B♭ [Bassoon solo; strings]   "Donald is ask'd what he can do to deserve his Mistress, he offers a trial of skill with Malcolm they fight, Malcolm is disarmed / previous to the fight Donald places the Ring on the finger of a Statue"
14. Allegro 2/4, D   "The Old Man satisfy'd with Malcolm and Donald, invites them into the house"
15. Andante 2/2, G   "Donald attempts to regain his Ring
    ♭VI   he is repulsed by the Statue
    g   the Statue comes down and follows him / she shews him the Ring informs him by having placed it on her finger he married her / she vanishes / Donald runs off distracted"

{ } denotes passages in the program not strictly followed by the score

Scene 4
16. Duet: Queen, Film, "When Time who steals our years away"* +

Scene 5
17. Largo cantabile 4/4, G "Enter Donald, melancholy [Haydn, Symphony no. 93, ii]
   Enter Isabel / she accuses him of neglect
   he informs her of what past with him and the Statue
   [Strings, bassoon solo] g the Statue appears [Haydn, Symphony no. 93, ii]
   the Statue shows him the Ring, and again claims him
   as her husband / the Figure disappears"
18. Moderato 4/4, d "Isabel is shocked at Donald's terror / approaches him
   he sinks into her arms / she endeavours to convey him off
   {they are met by the Hermit Austin who gives them a Talisman
   to break the charm}"
19. Allegro 2/4, F "they embrace and go in quest of the Fairies
   {Donald meets with the Fairies, shews them the Talisman,
   and the charm is broke. The Fairies disappear, the
   Scene flies to pieces, and discovers a magnificent
   FAIRY PALACE}"

Scene 6
"The Ballet concludes with Dances by the various Characters, Isabel, Donald &c."
[Tempo unmarked] 3/4, B♭ [Solo oboe and bassoon]
Minuetto 3/4, E♭-c-E♭ *Pas de trois*
Andante 4/4, B♭
Andante 2/4, B♭ *Pas seul*: Jane
[Tempo unmarked] 2/4, B♭ "The Old Man's Dance"—"Finale"

The plot concerns the union of mortal lovers Donald and Isabel and their acceptance into the fairy community. Fawcett also includes the well-worn device of a statue that comes to life, an idea which had been anticipated in *Don Giovanni* but which, in this instance, was borrowed from "The Ring," a poem by Thomas Moore, published in *Poetical Works of the late Thomas Little, Esq.* (Dublin: Carpenter, 1801). The scene is laid in the Scottish highlands and the score includes music in the Scots-style as well as authentic borrowings. The overture includes variations on the "Blue bells of Scotland," first played by two cellos and subsequently by two bassoons; these variations are repeated when Isabel dances for Donald. The statue comes to life accompanied by the cantabile theme from the second movement of Haydn's Symphony no. 93 (1791) and this makes very effective "ghost" music (Arnold employs Haydn's theme in its original G major and minor modes). Only the fairies are entrusted with singing parts so as to stress their difference from mortal beings.

The starred/crossed item was published separately (Hoskins, *Arnold*, 2:302-03; RISM AA2244a) and there is a manuscript copy in the Royal College of Music 2110 (S.H. 1948), f. 63b. A copy of the printed song-words and prospectus (London: Cadell and Davies, 1802) is in the University of Michigan Music Library; Larpent Ms. 1356.

F / Incidental Music

F1 **MACBETH**
William Shakespeare's play with Richard Leveridge's music (1702) and new instrumental entr'actes by Arnold
First performed at the Haymarket Little Theatre, 7 September 1778
Printed score (London: W. Warrell, ca. 1778; RISM A2285; scored for strings, flute, 2 oboes, bassoon, 2 horns, 2 trumpets, side drum, keyboard continuo)

    F1.1   March for *Macbeth* (strings, oboes, horns, trumpets, side drum, continuo)

    F1.2   "The birks of Endermay" [Invermay] preceding act 1 (strings, flute, horns, continuo)

    F1.3   "The yellow hair'd laddie" for the end of act 1 (strings, oboes, horns, continuo)

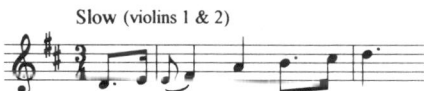

    F1.4   "The braes of Balandine" [Ballenden] for the end of act 2 (strings, oboes, bassoon, horns, continuo)

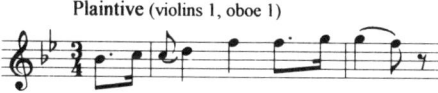

    F1.5   "Menuetto to be play'd at the banquet" (strings, oboes, horns, continuo)

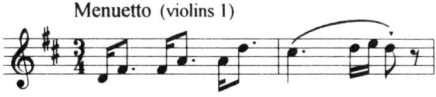

    F1.6   "Lochaber" for the end of act 3 (strings, flute, oboe, bassoon, continuo)

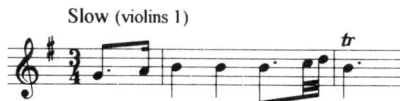

A Thematic Index

F1.7 "Earl of Douglas's lament" for the end of act 4 (strings, oboes, horns, continuo)

Slow and plaintive (violins 1, oboe 1)

F1.8 "The favorite march in Bonducca" (i.e. "Britons strike home" from Henry Purcell's *Bonduca*, 1695; strings, oboes, horns, trumpets, side drum, continuo

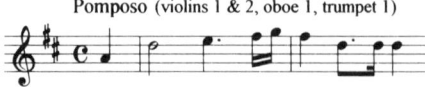

Pomposo (violins 1 & 2, oboe 1, trumpet 1)

To provide "location," five of the pieces are arrangements of Scottish folksongs; **F1.1** and **F1.5** are in quasi-Scots style. Only the first and last numbers employ ceremonial trumpets and side drum; for the rest, the orchestra is of modest proportions. There is a review of the Haymarket production in the *Morning Chronicle*, 8 September 1778, but no coverage of Arnold's music. My edition of Arnold's score is published by Artaria Editions, no. AE089 (Wellington, New Zealand, 1997).

F2   THE POSITIVE MAN
Farce in two acts
Libretto by John O'Keeffe, after his *The She Gallant* (1767)
First performed at Covent Garden, 16 March 1782

Incidental music for this work was provided by Michael Arne and William Shield with one song by Arnold for John Lee as Quid in act 1; this item makes its appearance in Arnold's pantomime *The Gnome*, in which it became popular (see **E7**). A copy of the libretto (London: T. Woodfall, 1798) is in the Bodleian Library: Vet.A5e.1640(7); Larpent Ms. 587.

F3   FATAL CURIOSITY

For George Colman, the elder's adaptation of George Lillo's domestic tragedy *Fatal Curiosity* (1736), performed at the Haymarket Little Theatre, 29 June 1782, Arnold re-set Maria's air in act 1; according to the *Morning Herald*, 30 June 1782, Miss Hooke sang it "very prettily." The song, strophic in form and in ballad style, tells of a maid whose lover has drowned; it begins:

F3.1   Affettuoso

Cease, cease heart ea - sing tears

(London: Longman & Broderip, 29 June 1782; RISM A2246)

There is a copy of the printed libretto (London: T. Cadell, 1783) in the Bodleian Library: 643.g.16(11); Larpent Ms. 595.

F4 THE TOBACCO BOX (THE SOLDIER'S PLEDGE OF LOVE)

This incidental interlude was first performed at the Haymarket Little Theatre on 13 August 1782, sharing a quadruple bill. According to Oulton, *Theatres*, 1:110, "The original music was French; the accompaniments were Dr. Arnold's." The piece takes the form of a dialogue in which Tom (William Brett), ordered to report to his regiment, bids farewell to Kate (Catherine Morris), and gives her his tobacco box as a keepsake; the lovers sing alternate stanzas to the same music and finally unite in unison. The words, possibly a translation by George Colman, the elder, were printed in the *Public Advertiser* of 19 August 1782. The song begins:

F4.1

(London: G. Walker, ca. 1790, copy in Lilly Library, Indiana University: M219.V157)

F5 A BEGGAR ON HORSEBACK
Farce in 2 acts
Libretto by John O'Keeffe
First performed at the Haymarket Little Theatre, 16 June 1785

For this work Arnold contributed a spirited patter song for John Edwin as Corney Buttercup (act 1). There are amusing verses about performing animals and these are set in courtly dance rhythms (minuet and allemande), which alternate with a refrain in rustic 6/8 meter. The song begins:

F5.1

(London: Harrison & Co., 1785; RISM A2216)

There is a copy of the printed libretto (London: T. Woodfall, 1798) in the Bodleian Library: Vet.A5e.1641(7); Larpent Ms. 699.

F6 HOW TO BE HAPPY
Comedy in 5 acts; music partially extant
Libretto by George Brewer
First performed at the Haymarket Little Theatre, 9 August 1794

F6.1   Miss Harcourt's song (act 3)

(London: Preston & Son, ca. 1794; RISM A2259)

Apart from this simple song supplied for Elizabeth Kemble, Arnold's incidental music is lost. The play lasted only three nights. *The Times*, 11 August 1794, noted "Mrs. Kemble warbled a plaintive air most sweetly" but disliked the rest of the music (including an "Irish" patter song and a "squall of a lullaby"). Larpent Ms. 1034.

F7   **THE WEDDING DAY**
Farce in 2 acts
Libretto by Elizabeth Inchbald
First performed at the Haymarket Little Theatre, 1 November 1794

This play entertained audiences nineteen times the first season and went on to become a stable of the repertory. Lady Contest, the heroine, was played by Dorothea Jordan, whose part included "In the dead of the night," a simple strophic song by Arnold which was sung originally as an independent song for the Vocal Concerts at Willis's Rooms in 1793 and later, to new words, in *Zorinski* (**B15**). The song appears in act 2 and the text deals with a favorite subject describing how Cupid does not find his mark; according to Jordan's biographer, James Broaden, *The Life of Mrs. Jordan* (London: E. Bull, 1831), 1:273, it "introduced one of the wonders of the ballad style and Cupid knocked at the window, very successfully, of every creature who heard her sing it." The air begins:

F7.1

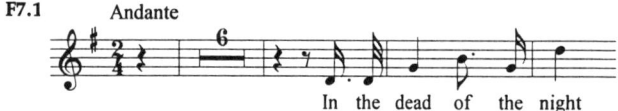

(London: n.p., 1794)

There were several English and American editions under the caption-title "As sung by Mrs. Jordan in the comedy of The Wedding Day"; see Edith B. Schnapper, *The British Union-Catalogue of Early Music*, 2 vols. (London: Butterworth Scientific Publications, 1957), 2:1061, and Oscar G. Sonneck, *A Bibliography of Early Secular American Music (18th Century)*, rev. William T. Upton (1945; reprint, New York: Da Capo, 1964), 95. A copy of the libretto (London: G. & J. Robinson, 1794) is in the Bodleian Library: Malone.B.46(5); Larpent Ms. 1044.

F8   **LOVE AND MADNESS! (THE TWO NOBLE KINSMEN)**
Tragi-comedy in 5 acts; music not extant

Libretto by Francis Godolphin Waldron (altered from William Shakespeare and John Fletcher, *The Two Noble Kinsmen*, 1634)
First performed at the Haymarket Little Theatre, 21 September 1795

The printed song-words (London: for the editor [Waldron], 21 September 1795; copy in the British Library: 11621.h.1(103)) reveals that six songs by Waldron to music by Arnold were sung by Sarah Harlowe as the Jailor's daughter, now named Hermia. There is no doubt that the character of the jailor's daughter in *The Two Noble Kinsmen*, driven to madness by unrequited love and taking recourse in singing snatches of song, derives from the theatrical vogue initiated by the role of Ophelia. Larpent Ms. 1094.

F9   **OPHELIA'S SONGS IN *HAMLET***

Shakespeare's play with the authentic Drury Lane tunes for the songs of Ophelia arranged by Arnold. Printed vocal score (London: J. & H. Caulfield, ca. 1801; copies in the Bodleian Library: Mus. 2c.240(24) and the British Library: G.383.h.(8)).

The following are settings of texts from act 5, scene 4:

F9.1
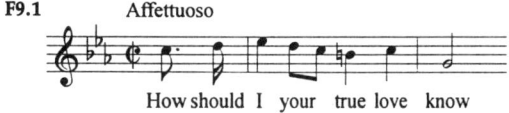

F9.2
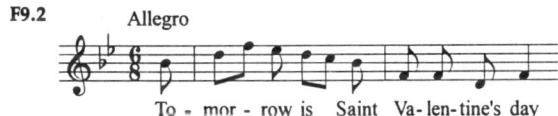

F9.3
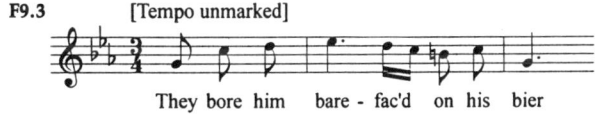

F9.4
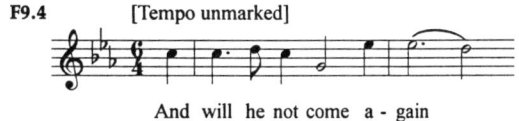

It appears that these melodies were copied down from the direction of Dorothea Jordan, who had played the role of Ophelia at Drury Lane between 29 April and 11 February 1799. The above edition is from Caulfield's *Vocal Music to Shakespeare's Plays*; the attribution to Arnold is found in the caption-title. For information concerning the airs upon which Arnold's arrangements are based, see Peter J. Seng's *The Vocal Music in the Plays of Shakespeare* (Cambridge: Harvard University Press, 1967), 131-56; see also Gooch and Thatcher, *Shakespeare Music*, 1:284, and Frederick W. Sternfeld, *Music in Shakespearean Tragedy* (London: Routledge and Kegan Paul, 1963; 2nd ed., 1967).

Index of Text Incipits

A clerk I was in London gay **B9**
A court is the fountain of honour **C13**
A coward mean as ever ran **B8**
A kiss my girl, your hand my boy **C10**
A Lady in fair Seville city **E9**
A lively young maiden of blooming eighteen **D12**
A master I have and I am his man **B5**
A mercer I am **B6**
A piper o'er the meadows straying **B15**
A pleasant trick **A12**
A poor little gipsy **C23, C28, C30**
A shepherd become **D10**
A soldier I am for a lady **B5**
A spruce little drummer **C30**
A voyage o'er seas **B9**
A yeoman of no mean degree **C18**
Abroad after misses most husbands will roam **D7**
Adieu, dearest friend **C16**
Adzooks old crusty **B6**
Against the rubs of life to guard **C31**
Ah how delighted will she be **B18**
Ah, how hapless is the maid **B2**
Ah madam, reflect **A6**
Ah parents, e'er your glass is run **B7**
Ah parents, ere your glass is run **B7**
Ah polite, debonaire **B8**
Ah, Solitude take my distress **B5**
Ah, fond lover, soothe my anguish **C13**
Ah, sweet Matilda stay **D12**
Ah, what's a valiant hero? **B10**
Ah, why take back the vows you gave **C10**
Ah? Basta! Bene Castruccina **A12**
Alas and woe to Fanny **A12**
All folks labour with disease **E4**
Amo, amas, I love a lass **C10**
An actor's a comical dog **C7**
An humble batchelor is nigh **B2**
And must I cruel fate resign **D3**
And shall I Jemmy's/Jenny's love retain **C24**
And will he not come again? **F9**
And will my love contented be **C30**
As t'other day in harmless chat **C32**

As the soldier lad **B11**
As through the clouds rolls rumbling thunder **B7**
As we goatherds trudge along **B14**
At an inn so merry **B6**
At court where true breeding abounds **D3**
At sixteen years old **B14**
At Symonds Inn I sip my tea **C25**
Auspicious pow'rs **B5**
Away sir, get out of my sight **C7**
Away to the woodlands **A4**
Away with all strife! **A6**
Away with tyrant laws that check **D6**
Away you wild inconstant lover **C4**

Bacchus is a jolly boy **C30**
Begone vain fool **C19**
Better to doubt **D7**
Bewailing, bewailing she sunk **B14**
Billy Bristle scorns to rank **C15**
Black Ladies and Gentlemen **E9**
Blind Cupid's darts **C14**
Bobbing about to the fiddle **B6**
Brave boys prepare **D7**
Briskly, briskly beat the hollow drum **C30**
Brother goatherd mark you me? **B14**
But see, unhappy omens **C31**
But see, the window opens **A12**
But who shall be the bearer of this letter? **A12**

Can I know from whence arise **D4**
Can words express **D7**
Can you cure master doctor, a very bad hand? **E4**
Cast my love thine eyes around **C5**
Cease, cease heart easing tears **F3**
Cheer up my lads **D7**
Come and crown your Billy's wishes **C15**
Come buy, who'll buy **C26**
Come follow, my lords and ladies gay **B8**
Come now begin **A12**
Come my lasses, let's be gay **D2**
Come Polly let's be gay **C25**

Index of Text Incipits

Come shipwrecked sailor C31
Come to the east E11
Come ye little dog C31
Come ye venal slaves of war B3
Come, cheer up my lads E4
Come, let us dance and sing B9
Come, little Tippet B6
Confound your noises! A12
Consult this joy-flush'd cheek C31
Cou'd you to battle march away B12
Courteous stranger B15
Cupid, God of pleasing anguish E1

Dame Nature in forming B5
Dark was the night B16
Dear is the incense that repentance flings B17
Dear wife forgive C16
Despair is all folly D7
Divino! 'tis the music of the spheres A12
Do thou, sweet sympathy, my voice convey B11
Drifted snow no more is seen B10
Dungeons and fetters may restrain B2
Duty is Nature's strongest law D3

Egad, we had a glorious feast C16
England, to thyself be true B10
Ere the lark's early carols C24
Ere the sun lifts his head E5
Erin and Albion, sister isles B5
Erst when my lovely Jane C19
Excuse me, my dear, but I think you conceited D12

Fain I'd see my Lydia fair C32
Faint and wearily the way-worn traveller B14
Fair Kitty gave to all delight D12
Farewell all hope of bliss! D7
Fate her forms at length redressing C19
Fell sorrow's gone by, dull gloom is dispersing D12
Fetch the keys good Master Shark C26
Flash lightnings, roll thunder E5
Flow thou regal purple stream B5
Flutt'ring, flutt'ring spread thy purple pinions A12
Fond maids like courtiers D7
For thee within my bosom D1
Fortune's like a tight or slip-shoe C15
Fresh and strong the breeze is blowing B9
From branch to branch C14
From fair London city C14
From this happy day B18

Give me back my heart, seducer! D2
Glitt'ring trifle sport of fashion C16
Go high, go low B3
Go wild and fickle rover B8
God save great George our king E4
Goddess of the magic cestus C4
Good Massa we find E9
Goodbye my fellow devils dear B15
Grateful Manteo is thy name D12
Great news! What? Pray good Bobby tell us D12
Great Sir consider C18

Ha! Are you there? A12
Hail! mighty king B15
Hail, happy people now rejoice C13
Hang care and drive sorrow away A6
Hang your humdrum loobies! B6
Hark the sprightly sounds begin B3
Hark, hark the village bells C31
Hark, hark 'tis the linnet E6
Hark where the trumpet now calls you to arms E4
Harry came to me last week C32
Haste my lads your lasses bring E1
Have I sav'd this girl and boy C18
Haul, haul away B3
He that weds a beauty D7
Hear, Julian, hear B13
Hence away with dismay C32
Here are catches, songs and glees C32
Here is a day, a day of wonders D12
Here lives sweet Castruccina! A12
Here quickly strike the strings B13
Here we sing, dance and play C10
Here we the sons of freedom dwell B5
His presence gives birth E5
Hist! Hist! I hear my mother call B1
Hither from our cloud top't mountains B17
Honour calls me from my arms D7
Honour plays a bubble's part D7
Hope still greets me C25
Hope, thou balm and source of pleasure C26
Hopes, doubts and fears C21
How calm her life B16
How can you be so teazing? D7
How clumsy the airs of a cit B6
How happy the woman B6
How hard our hapless lot B3
How keen the glance B11
How shall I begin it well C31

INDEX OF TEXT INCIPITS

How shou'd I your true love know F9
How sweetly glide the minutes o'er D12
How vain is caution C19
How will I play the lover's part A6
Hymen's delights they wish to prove D12

I can shoe a horse C14
I hate the foolish elf D7
I have lost her B11
I laugh, I dance, I pipe C14
I like the plain song C4
I ne'er knew a lady B18
I saw a stout fellow C14
I simply wait for your commands, Sir D6
I tremble to think that my soldier so bold B12
I will have my manners D7
Idalian queen to thee we pray B5
If a coxcomb all starch B6
If balmy friendship yet survives C7
If fondly thou dost not mistake C8
If happiness thro' me they gain D4
If husbands wish for happy lives B3
If I'm the happy man B3
If 'tis joy to wound a lover A1, C5
I'm a braw and bonny youth C19
I'm parish clerk and sexton here C30
I'm pretty, I'm pretty A6
I'm worse than poor debtors B7
In air, serenata A12
In an old quiet parish B10
In choice of a husband C10
In dear little Ireland C26
In fancy let nature delight B8
In gratitude to thy exalted friendship C4
In his ambush wisely dark B11
In Jacky Bull C10
In love and life the present use D7
In May fifteen hundred eighty and eight B8
In my clubroom so great C25
In my eyes dear Edward read C32
In the course of my life C27
In the dead of the night B15, F7
In the prattling hours of youth B3
In this dilemma, what can I say Sir D12
In vain to smother love we strive C7
Is that a form or feature A6
It's Polly asks, can you deny? C25

Jealous ears with whispers filling B2
Jocund fill the flowing bowl B7

John tripp'd up the stairs B6
Jonothan a-wooing went B7
Justice long forbearing D7

King Arthur kept at merry Carlisle B17
Knives to grind! A12

Ladies and gentlemen, this is a set B3
Lead on Gagliardo E10
Leander was my daily theme A6
Let envy, care and tumult cease C16
Let genuine pleasures here preside C31
Let me but my Caroline guard C7
Let not love B3
Let others complain E10
Let the loud ratt'ling drum B15
Let the swell of harmony B18
Let us all forgive the past C32
Let women love water C26
Let's all sit down to supper boys B8
List, little Fibby B7
Little thinks the townsman's wife B12
London ladies walk the streets B6
Look back, behold D2
Look maids! I cock my hat B7
Look, neighbours, look E4
Lord, what care I for mam and dad? C10
Lorenza rich and high in power B18
Love, jealousy, jealousy, rage D4
Love no toil regarding B16
Love with beauty is flying D7
Love's a spark D3
Love's a tender timid passion D12
Love, the soul firing B2
Low at your feet, we thus entreat A6
Lurk o'er the greensward B10
Lye still my heart, oh fatal stroke B1

Maidens do not think me stupid C4
Make room for a jolly stone-eater E7
Mark the hue of the lily C19
Mark the true test of passion C18
Mars wou'd oft his conquests B9
Merry are the bells C16
Mild aurora softly smiling C31
Mortal, mortal, mortal man B13
My bottle is my wife and friend C14
My comrades so famish'd and queer B12
My cruel love to danger go E9
My daddy was a good fellow B8
My dawn of life C13

161

Index of Text Incipits

My father Pan when I was born   B13
My fond heart sweetly basks   C14
My heart forbodes he's dead   D7
My heart is by love forsaken   D7
My Laura, wilt thou trust the seas   C10
My master a gay pulpiteer   B7
My tight fellow soldiers   B10
My wife in rage will rattle   B13

Near yonder hamlet   C23
Neatest of pretty feet   B3
Neighbours, neighbours, once in a way   E4
No lav'rocks e'er so sweetly sung   C19
No longer a ninny   B15
No longer Cupid's foe   C4
No more my fate is cast, fond hope adieu   D12
No sport to the chace can compare   D3
Non termer   A12
Nor wealth, nor birth, nor skill, nor pow'r   D12
Now Cynthia rode in silver car   B11
Now let joy and mirth go round   C25
Now my flocks have gone   C19
Now the storms of life are over   C26

O 'tis mighty delightful   C25
O curse your din you've shut me in   A12
O let me in those ringlets stray   B13
O listen then and silent feel   C25
O the face of brave Captain Megan   C32
O the ton the dear ton   C2
O thou whose charms   A12
O when the liquor I do quaff   B13
O'er the ocean when sailors are roaming   C26
Observe the statesman's ways   D7
Odds life when a sailor   C31
Of all the evils   A6
Of all the pretty flowers   C10
Of love, sweet love   C16
Of wine, of wine   C2
Off, you dog, or I'll crack your crown   B11
Oh dear, oh dear   D12
Oh follow, then, where Nonsense points the way   E4
O happy tawny Moor   B14
Oh how could you leave your own Jenny   C19
Oh how painful 'tis to part   A6
Oh how sweetly pleasure's tasted   C10
Oh let me ne'er for fortune pine   C24
Oh say, simple maid   B9
Oh the joys of wedded life   C19

Oh the moment was sad   B12
Oh vat a happy day   A12
Oh, whack, cupid's a mannikin   C30
Oh when I was a little fool   B8
Oh where e're you chance to rove   E4
Oh, yeo! Oh, yeo! Heave the anchor   C19
Old father McShane   B18
On board the Valiant   C26
On our green tambourine   B18
Once in a chimney corner snug   B7
Once on a time   B6
Only look at me maids   B7
Other maidens bait their hooks   B16
Our cares are all vanish'd   E1
Our grotto was the sweetest place   B9

Painful to part   A12
Paphian bowers   C16
Past six o'clock   E4
Patriots at first aloud declare   D7
Peace to the heroes   B12
Pensive I mourn my absent swain   B6
Pretty Moggy, cease I pray   C19
Prythee ope your cottage door   C26

Quashee he load his gun   E9
Quick for a smile implore me   C13

Rear our English banner high   B12
Remember when we walk'd alone   B9
Rude the wind, unkind the show'r   F6
Ruin seize thee, ruthless king   B17

Save me, save me, white man save me   D12
Secure in my Maria's heart   C14
See a nymph so brisk and witty   C7
See brother, see on yonder bough   C18
See Flora's bowers   B8
See Lady Tonish   C14
See the blossom of spring   C7
See the stream so smoothly sliding   C24
September the thirteenth   C14
Shall I not be bold   D7
She who hath felt a real pain   D7
Sickly dotage to restrain   B2
Signor Cranky then addio   C4
Signor, signor   B5
Silence Welch goats?   A12
Silence, take notice, you're my song   E5

Simplicity, thou fav'rite child **B9**
Since I feel I'm growing old **C15**
Since that clear day **C14**
Sing tingering **E9**
Sir Solomons Simons **C16**
Smile, kindest fortune **B6**
Smiths are good fellows **E5**
Social pow'rs at pleasures call **B5**
Soft Arno's stream **C14**
Some like great bowls to quaff **C10**
Some talk of Cherokees Sir **B7**
Sound, sound the solemn strains and slow **B12**
Strike, strike, strike **B10**
Sturdily the tempest howling **C26**
Such beauties in view **C10**
Sulky pride dare not here venture **B13**
Sure 'twould make a dismal story **C5**
Swear by the silver crescent of the night **E9**
Sweet content can banish strife **C13**
Sweet girls, don't depend **B8**
Sweet ladies, look, admire, behold **B8**
Sweet mercy is the loveliest flow'r **D3**
Sweetest passion of the mind **C13**
Swell aloud the conquering strain **C31**

Talk not of your dirty acres **B6**
Tell-tale eyes **B2**
Ten thousand times around the globe **E5**
Than envied monarchs happier still **B15**
That passion which harrows **D3**
The Achilles, tho' christen'd **B9**
The beacon flames, the Turks are come **B8**
The bells are begun **B1**
The bloom of inexperienced youth **C29**
The body of the brave may be taken **D7**
The crow or daw thro' all the year **D7**
The deuce o' one **C16**
The guns proclaim some strangers near **D12**
The hardy sailor braves the ocean **B5**
The Irish you shall find **E5**
The ladies cannot but approve **E7**
The man whose life is on the seas **C25**
The manners of the great affect **D7**
The mincing step **B10**
The morning breeze which sweeps the grove **B11**
The music's prepar'd **C14**
The musk rose blooms in thorns and tears **B5**
The night comes on without a star **B8**
The sailor who ploughs the salt wave **C31**
The quarrels of lovers **B1**

The slender waist **C16**
The soldier in his calm retreat **C16**
The soldiers, who by trade must dare **D7**
The sportsmen keep hawks **D7**
The stag when chas'd **D7**
The storm arose, the ship was lost **C31**
The study intense **B6**
The sun is sunk **B14**
The sun sets at night **B11**
The sun was set, the night was grey **B17**
The sweet kiss of my dear **B18**
The tuneful lark **C10**
The turtle thus upon the spray **D7**
The virgin lily of the night **C10**
The wand'ring sailor **B3**
The white man comes **E9**
The world is all nonsense and noise **C7**
The world is always jarring **D7**
Then away with all care **C7**
Then come indoors to make love **B6**
Then if our friends and patrons here **C24**
There is a chambermaid **B6**
There lies your road, sweet sir adieu **D2**
There lives a maid at Wapping Wall **B8**
There to muse and there to sigh **B11**
There was Dorothy Dump **C18**
They bore him barefac'd on his bier **F9**
Think your tawny Moor is true **B14**
This face observe discerning fair **C4**
This maxim let ev'ryone hear **B9**
This note tells Castruccina **A12**
Tho' different passions rage by turns **D7**
Tho' doom'd to tempt the fickle sea **A6**
Tho' lovers, like marksmen, all aim at the heart **B9**
Tho' not in the bloom of my youth **A6**
Tho' sweetly breathes the smiling spring **C4**
Tho' the fate of battle **F4**
Tho' the lawyer comes to woo **C25**
Tho' the pit my son has swallow'd **E3**
Tho' the warm and youthful dame **E4**
Tho' years glide away **B18**
Thou hast play'd **B3**
Thou sandy bourne **B11**
Thou that liv'st in every port **B11**
Though my dress perhaps is homely **B8**
Three pilgrims at love's sacred shrine **B11**
Thus my boys, our anchor's weigh'd **C10**
Till now the heav'ns were my guide **D4**
Tis pleasant to see when my lord obtains **B11**
Tis thus with a wife **E4**

Index of Text Incipits

Tis true I'm a fright **E3**
To arms, to arms, when captains cry **B10**
To bid adieu to her I love **D12**
To ease my heart **B3**
To heal the wound a bee had made **E3**
To shun the gay and gaudy bow'r **B11**
To win all the fair ones **B17**
Tom Clueline, Ben Bowling **C31**
Tomorrow is Saint Valentine's day **F9**
Twas I learn't a pretty song in France **E5**
Twas on a pleasant summer's morn **B15**
Twas on Christmas day **C19**
Two maidens my heart transfix'd **B11**

Uncertainty with chequer'd crew **B6**
Under elms umbrageous lying **B13**

Victory is ours **D7**
Virtue's treasure **D7**

Wampum sampum **B9**
Wander now to and fro **E9**
War, war, war has still its melody **B12**
Water parted from the sea **C4**
We love Massa **E9**
We Negro men and women **E9**
We never blame the forward swain **D7**
We the sword of valour drawing **D7**
Welcome Love, welcome Joy **E10**
Welcome, sweet fancy **B6**
Well I know thou friendly stream **D4**
What are Pluto's gilded toys **D10**
What boots it where thy soldier lies **B11**
What causes my Donald this pain **E11**
What citadel so proud can say **B9**
What is a poet sir? **C12**
What man can virtue or courage repose **D7**
What means that downcast look **B3**
What pleasure to think **C16**
What shall I do, oh dear, oh dear **D6**
What should sailors do on shore? **E7, F2**
What sweet sensation **B8**
What tho' fine ladies **C32**
When a lady of ton **B3**
When a lover's in the wind **B6**
When a maid in way of marriage **B1**
When a man like myself **C31**
When a woman jealous grows **D7**
When alas my true love left me **B18**
When Arthur first in court **B10**

When beaus and smarts **A6**
When billows are breaking **D7**
When blest with my Jemmy **C24**
When cruel parents **B6**
When cruising off Brest **C25**
When e'er a lover sighs **B7**
When e'er the evening dew descends **B7**
When first an Arragonian maid **C13**
When first I saw my Susan's face **C19**
When first this little heart began **B15**
When first to Helen's lute **C18**
When gold is in hand **D7**
When I left Primrose Green **C7**
When I to London first came in **C19**
When I was a boy **B17**
When I was a younker **C16**
When I was at home **B12**
When kings by their huffing **D7**
When love gets you fast in her clutches **C18**
When lovers are old **A6**
When madam **B3**
When miss's lover's call'd away **B18**
When on board the Hector **C25**
When on the ocean **C26**
When storms are sunk to rest **C31**
When the blithe village maids **B11**
When the chace of day is done **B9**
When the hollow drum **B14**
When the lark in æther singing **C30**
When the rude voice of war **B17**
When the stout freebooters prowl **B10**
When the tyger roams **D7**
When Time who steals our years away **E11**
When with tenderness we languish **B2**
When women are partners at cards **C32**
When you discover **B18**
While pert cock sparrows sport and play **C7**
While the hideous night is scowling **B15**
White man never go away **B9**
Who in absence long have known **B11**
Who wou'd not up to London come **F5**
Who'd believe that did not hear **D12**
Why did Damon's eyes so bright **B7**
Why did you spare him **D7**
Why shou'd I vain fears discover **B9**
Wine, wine is the liquor of life **B2**
With a heart light and gay **C26**
With an air debonair **C4**
With arms across **C8**
With honour's scars **C14**

INDEX OF TEXT INCIPITS

With many a sad, intrusive doubt oppress'd **B11**
With these happy tidings fraught **D2**
Without a man to take the lead **B3**
Woman's like the flatt'ring ocean **D7**
Wou'd you know how you must find it **B13**

Ye freeborn sons Britannia's boast **C21**
Ye nymphs and sylvan Gods **A12**
Yes thou goddess fair and free **E4**
Yes I'll die an old maid **C31**
Yes, yes, he has landed **E9**
You high-born Spanish noblemen **B14**
You love and are belov'd again **D2**
You may slight me who's afraid **B7**
You my spruce little Mathew **B7**

You never hear of Mandingo king **E9**
You that join our mighty trade **B13**
You'll wonder sage doctor **E1**
You're so charming and fair **C4**
Young Moggy and Peggy **D12**
Young Simon in his lovely Sue **C18**
Your colinets and arietts **B9**
Your lordship is welcome **C16**
Your master, young man, may a lass adore **B7**
Your toupee I can twirl **B2**
Your wife men all declare **B8, C13**
Your worship your wings may clap **C16**
Youth will not return **E4**

Zounds, rascal speak out **B2, C9**

About the Author

ROBERT H. B. HOSKINS, *M.A. from the University of Canterbury, and Ph.D. at the University of Auckland, is Senior Lecturer in Music at Massey University, New Zealand. He is the author of three books on colonial balladry, and his work on eighteenth-century English theater music has appeared in* New Grove, New Grove Opera, Studies in Music, Music for London Entertainment, 1660-1800, *and the* Blackwell History of Music in Britain. *He is co-editor of the New Zealand Musicological Society's* Research Chronicle, *and series editor of Massey University Music publications specializing in works by New Zealand composers. He has recently edited Arnold's extant orchestral music for Artaria Editions. He has a wife, Cecily, a teacher, and a daughter, Polly, aged 2.*